The Multicultural Riddle

Zones of Religion

Peter van der Veer, editor

Previously published in the series:

Conversion to Modernities
Peter van der Veer

Border Fetishisms
Patricia Spyer

Appropriating Gender
Patricia Jeffery and Amrita Basu

The Multicultural Riddle

Rethinking National, Ethnic, and Religious Identities

GERD BAUMANN

ROUTLEDGE

New York and London

The Multicultural Riddle

Rethinking National, Ethnic, and Religious Identities

GERD BAUMANN

ROUTLEDGE

New York and London

Published in 1999 by
Routledge
29 West 35th Street
New York, NY 10001

Published in Great Britain by
Routledge
11 New Fetter Lane
London EC4P 4EE

Copyright © 1999 by Routledge

Printed in the United States of America on acid-free paper.

Library of Congress Cataloging-in-Publication Data

The multicultural riddle : rethinking national, ethnic, and religious identities / Gerd Baumann.
        p. cm. — (Zones of religion)
    Includes bibliographical references and index.
    ISBN 0-415-92212-7 (hc.) — ISBN 0-415-92213-5 (pbk.)
    1. Ethnicity. 2. Multiculturalism. 3. Human rights. 4. Civil rights. 5.
Religion and culture.   I. Title.   II. Series.
GN495. 6. B38   1999
305.8—dc21   98–49911
                                                                  CIP

Contents

About This Book

A RIDDLE IS A PARADOX that can be solved by rethinking the terms in which it is posed. When Oedipus was asked what walks on four legs in the morning, on two legs at noon, and on three at night, he cracked this famous "Riddle of the Sphinx" by rethinking the meaning of the riddle's crucial term. A leg meant any support on the ground—toddlers move on all fours, adults walk on two legs, and the old may use a walking stick—thus the riddle was about human beings, and the day was their lifetime. The answer seems simple, but it required rethinking the terms of the question. Multiculturalism, too, is a riddle. It asks how we can establish a state of justice and equality between and among three parties: those who believe in a unified national culture, those who trace their culture to their ethnic identity, and those who view their religion as culture. To solve the riddle, one needs to rethink what is meant by nationality or the nation-state, by ethnic identity or ethnicity, and by religion as a basis of culture. What all three acts of rethinking have in common is a new concern with the meaning and making of culture. Multiculturalism is not the old concept of culture multiplied by the number of groups that exist, but a new, and internally plural, praxis of culture applied to oneself and to others. This is what this book tries to show.

The Multicultural Riddle

The book is concerned with North America and Europe for two reasons. First, these two parts of "the West" have been in constant interchange about the meaning of the multicultural riddle: They are like two, or maybe two hundred, different people who are busy with the same riddle, each trying to solve it their own way. Comparing their approaches allows us to study the riddle in all its different contexts, for as we will see, there is no such thing as a multicultural society within the boundaries of one nation-state. Secondly, the multicultural riddle is North American in its origins, but the most varied attempts to tackle it are found in Europe. To say this is not to adjudicate high grades in virtue, but to point to some astonishing historical shifts between the two continents. An alertness to comparison is the lifeblood of all multicultural thinking.

The first ideal readers I kept in mind for this book were my second-year students in political anthropology at the University of New Mexico. Two further rounds of student critique at Brunel University, London, and the University of Amsterdam convinced me that the third multicultural focus, on religion, should be sharpened by concentrating on one faith. I have chosen Islam in the West because this is the most contentious and thus the most revealing site of the multicultural riddle across the two continents. The ideal critics for the first and second draft were my colleagues at the Research Centre Religion and Society of the University of Amsterdam. I thank Peter van der Veer, Patricia Spyer, Peter van Rooden, Birgit Meyer, and Peter Pels. I further thank Marie-Benedicte Dembour (Sussex University), Marie Gillespie and Tom Cheesman (Swansea University), Steven Vertovec (Oxford University), and Bryan Mohamed (Rietveld Academy, Amsterdam), as well as the staff at Routledge, all of whom gave me their generous help and advice.

For ease of use, the literature is divided into two parts: There are some two hundred references that I have used and therefore need to credit at the end, and there are recommendations for further reading appended to each chapter. I have been ruthless in keeping these short to guarantee page-for-page value: When there was no summary article, I have selected only parts of the best books I know. I thus recommend the *Further Reading* sections to anyone who wants to come to their own conclusions in this search for the basics of multicultural thinking.

Gerd Baumann
Research Centre Religion & Society
The University of Amsterdam

1

"I Have a Dream"—
but Who Is It For?

Civil Rights, Human Rights, or Community Rights?

> So I say to you, my friends, that even though we must face the
> difficulties of today and tomorrow, I still have a dream. It is a
> dream deeply rooted in the American dream that one day this
> nation will rise up and live out the true meaning of its creed—
> we hold these truths to be self-evident that all men are created
> equal. . . . I have a dream my four little children will one day
> live in a nation where they will not be judged by the color of
> their skin but by content of their character. I have a dream
> today! . . . I have a dream . . . that one day, right there in
> Alabama, little black boys and black girls will be able to join
> hands with little white boys and white girls as sisters and
> brothers. I have a dream today! (King [1963] 1968, 16–17)

MARTIN LUTHER KING's vision of a future without ethnic or cultural discrimination is rightly regarded as programmatic for the
past thirty years and the next fifty. Its sentiments have been
echoed in dozens of struggles across the globe to obtain equality
for all, regardless of ethnic, cultural, or religious differences.

Whether this meant equality in treatment, rights, recognition, life chances, or success was a moot question then. Yet in hindsight, King rallied the troops, but they did not follow his strategy. The leader of the Civil Rights Movement wanted exactly that: equal rights based on civil rights, that is, based on the premise of equal and individual citizenship. In some ways, this line of argument had been overtaken even as it was being cast into its visionary form. The struggle against ethnic or cultural discrimination took on an entirely different logic within a few years of King's murder: The Civil Rights Movement lost its combative edge to the Black Consciousness Movement, and this and its many successors put forth a different argument altogether—discrimination, and for that matter emancipation, was not a question of individual civil rights, but of collective rights, that is, rights assigned to groups, be they real or imagined. There were two transformations in this process.

The first transformation was to translate present-day civil rights, that is, the rights of citizens regardless of color, religion, or parents' culture, into ethnic rights.[1] The most outspoken of these ethnic translations was the Black Power Movement, concerned not with the rights of Americans as such, but with the rights of African Americans as a community. This community had to be styled into a community of culture, as well as color, but the act of restyling failed on two counts: On the inside, there were too many people who refused to develop a specifically "black" consciousness, rather than an American one or a Christian one. From the outside, the nation as a whole was slow in coming to terms with community, as opposed to individual, rights.

The next transformation was to translate ethnic community rights into religious community rights, and this translation drew on very different symbolic resources. Its protagonists revived the memory of Noble Drew Ali in the 1910s and Elijah Muhammad in the 1930s, two of the founders of a new African American Islam in the United States. With the slow progress of both civil and ethnic rights, religious community rights took on a new significance for two reasons—again, one external and one internal. Externally, the political elites of the United States could not be seen to condone inequality on the basis of religion. Internally, religion could be advertised, not only as a reason to get collective rights but also as a means to deserve them: "In reflection on the struggle of African Americans against racism, . . . [Islam serves as a new] foundation that reforms the character of the individual toward traits necessary for success. . . . There is a [new] focus on establishing belief and the principles which will lay the foundation for education and self-sufficiency" (McCloud 1995, 88–89). From Malcolm X in the 1960s to Louis Farrakhan in the 1990s, the most audible rallying cries were thus not addressed to American citizens as such or to an ethnic group as such. Rather, they were addressed to an emergent new "nation," the Nation of Islam, which was to lead African Americans out of the false "American" nation of white Christian oppressors.

Evidently, these three approaches do not mark three separate periods in history. The Civil Rights Movement has not suddenly stopped: Witness the campaigns for ethnic voter registration and the politics of Jesse Jackson and other Democrats. There are plenty of remnants both of the civil rights approach and of the ethnic rights approach. No one can know about their relative success in the future. What matters, however, is this: There are three kinds of rights that multiculturalists can fight for, but they are not the same kinds of rights.

The differences between them are crucial, and they lie at the heart of the multicultural riddle almost everywhere. Discrimination, as well as forced or expected assimilation, can be fought on three platforms, but each platform defines different allies and adversaries, as well as different insiders and outsiders. Discrimination can be fought on the civil rights platform because it means inequality among citizens. Alternatively, it can be fought because, and insofar as, it means inequality among ethnic groups

3

or among religious groups. Since these groups of cocitizens, coethnics, and coreligionists have different boundaries, and since they use different arguments to fight inequality, they seek different kinds of equality. Civil rights movements exclude foreigners, ethnic rights movements exclude so-called non- or half-ethnics, and religious rights movements exclude nonbelievers.

The differences between these kinds of rights would not be so worrisome if there were some ultimate kind of right to which proponents of all three could appeal. Such a superlogic of rights does indeed seem to exist, and it is known as human rights. Let us see, therefore, whether the ideology of human rights can serve to unite the proponents of civil, ethnic, and religious rights.

To call human rights an ideology, rather than a logic, may sound cynical at first sight. Ideology, after all, is the word for a kind of self-interested and wishful (non)thinking. But there are good reasons for this, both cultural-historical and present-day legal. To show their cultural-historical specificity, one may think of the human rights debates in the United Nations. Whenever democratic states chastise police states for their violations of human rights, the answer rings loud and clear: "Human rights talk is Western cultural imperialism! It is foreign interference in another state's internal affairs." Admittedly, this kind of argument usually comes from privileged fat-cat diplomats, not from the victims of human rights violations. The victims, be they oppressed minorities or political prisoners, child laborers or women not treated as the equals of men, would probably want their human rights to be universally valid. Yet state elites can reject them whenever it suits them, and they do so by pointing to their cultural-historical specificity.

A more credible critique of the human rights concept can be advanced from within the Western framework itself, and it shows that human rights are neither universal, nor even rights. To dig up their cultural-historical roots, one may best consult the great Thomas Paine, the first truly international radical, who coinspired the American Constitution, the French Revolution, and other democratic movements right across the West. In his famous treatise, *The Rights of Man* (1791), Tom Paine argued in a deliberately multicultural way: "*Every* history of the creation, and *every* traditionary account, whether from the lettered or the unlettered world, however they may vary in their opinion or belief of certain particulars, all agree in establishing one point: THE UNITY OF MAN; by which I mean that, all men are born equal, and with equal natural right" (Conway 1967, 304; capitals in original; italics mine). This is a fine thing to believe, but all the evidence we have goes against it: From the book of Genesis to the creation myths of thousands of "unlettered," that is, oral, cultures, we see creation imagined as a hierarchical process, be it between the genders or between ethnic groups, between believers and pagans or between nobles and commoners. Paine himself knew this perfectly well, and to get out of the fix, he had to invent a new philosophy of creation that even denied the relevance of having sex.[2] Given such difficulties in arguing, or even willing, human rights, one must admire the wisdom of the American Constitution, echoed in the speech of King, which simply calls equality a "self-evident truth." But what is self-evident in one culture may look very far-fetched in another, and while the idea of human rights may be a wonderfully fine ideology, it is an ideology none the less.

Apart from the historical and cultural reasons for calling it so, there are very hard legal reasons too. The best examination of these reasons comes from Marie-Benedicte Dembour, an anthropologist as well as a lecturer in international law. Dembour (1996) indeed uses the word "ideology" herself; as a lawyer she must admit that "human rights are first and foremost political aspirations. . . . [T]he effectiveness of human rights at an individual level depends on the person belonging to the "right" national state, [and even then] their practice excludes whole classes of people" (Dembour 1996, 18–19). We end up with the same sad conclusion that we faced in United Nations diplomacy, only this time on better authority: Human rights can only be enjoyed within the boundaries set by nation-states, and nation-states are even worse at protecting human rights than they are at guaranteeing civil rights. The record is bad.

Dembour gives two very poignant examples of people excluded from human rights by national laws: It is left up to every nation-state to interpret whether a migrant is classified as an "economic migrant" (usually thrown out) or a "political refugee" (sometimes let in). It is also left up to every nation-state to restrict the rules under which a recognized political refugee is granted the "universal human right" of political asylum. But more than that, matters are just as bad for those who want to, or can, stay at home. The United Nations Declaration of Human Rights (1948) is just that: a declaration of fine intentions, but certainly "not binding in law" (Donnelly 1989, 14; Dembour 1996, 28). The only human rights treaty that is indeed binding in law, the European Convention on Human Rights (1950), again proves the old adage of the law as an ass: The ultimate legal authorities often "disagree whether facts submitted to them [may or may not] constitute violations of human rights guaranteed by the European Convention" (Dembour 1996, 36n. 15).

Neither Dembour nor I, nor any of the commentators I know, disagree with the moral value of "thinking" human rights. Dembour makes a passionate plea to cast away our ambivalence toward the idea, and Donnelly, who calls all human rights claims "essentially extralegal" (1989, 14) even tried out a Thomas Paine–like construction of "human dignity" to find some universal, culturally neutral, common ground (Donnelly 1982). But wish as we may, and dream as we must, the super-logic of human rights remains an ideology in every way. Historically and culturally, it rests on mythical thinking, however well intentioned; legally, it remains subject to the powers of nation-state elites, however well intentioned or selfish. What

6

human rights we may have, we can only enforce by the grace of our nation-states, and all that a government needs to renege on them is an obedient police force within, an effective immigration "service" at its borders, and a lying diplomat at the United Nations. If we had hoped that the logic of human rights might somehow render civil rights, ethnic rights, and religious liberties the same, we have bet on a lame horse. This, at least, is the lawyers' advice. We thus keep in hand three logics of equality that differ fundamentally. One is based on individualist, but legally enforceable, civil rights; the second on ethnic identity; and the third on religious equality. Let us therefore review these three kinds of rights briefly.

Civil rights are legally enforceable claims of a citizen, that is, not a person as such, but a person with a particular passport or national status. The idea has its roots in the ancient Greek city-states and in the Roman Empire state, but civil rights were hardly distinguishable in these contexts from ethnic or religious rights. Their reinvention for modern times was one of the great achievements of critical thinkers around 1750. These thinkers, among them John Locke and Tom Paine in Britain and Charles Montesquieu and Jean-Jacques Rousseau in France, invented the idea of a basic social contract between individuals and the state. This contract was envisaged as individuals giving up certain rights to the state and receiving selected other rights in return. Give up your right to carry a gun, and you get the right to be protected by a policeman; give up your right to sleep around, and gain the right to have your marriage protected by law. To have rights was thus the result of a deal: Natural persons join a state and give up natural rights; natural persons become citizens and get civil rights in return. If civil rights fail to respect people's natural rights, citizens have the right to overturn their government.

To us, of course, it is obvious that we are dealing with a philosophical fiction. What these thinkers confused, but confused quite deliberately to win the argument, was human society in general and the state in particular. We do, of course, surrender some of our desires to society at large: Most of us call that "civilization," and it leads to ideas about self-control, public and private property, and the peaceful resolution of conflicts. But compromising to live in human society is, nonetheless, something different than subordinating oneself to a state. What the Enlightenment thinkers tried to do with this line of arguing was to demote the state and all its might to acting as a mere servant of the common good. They deliberately confused the nation-state with governance in general, the better to cut the state down to size. The great advantage was to reduce the state to being a partner in a social bargain. To honor that bargain, states had to render civil rights enforceable in the courts and promise all citizens equal treatment by all its powers. All citizens who enjoy civil rights must be equal before the lawmakers, or legislature; before the judges of the law, or jurisdiction; and before the executive and civil service. Despite its checkered argument, the civil rights approach is thus not to be discounted in the struggle for equality.

As a sole platform, however, it looks insufficient. There are tens of millions of illegal immigrants in the Western states, and there are tens of millions of legal immigrants who, nonetheless, are not nationals and are thus denied full civil rights. Neither of these groups will simply go back to where they originated, either because they have even fewer civil rights in their countries of birth or because Western economies make very good use of them. On top of that, there are tens of millions of full-status nationals living in their own Western countries that have been prevented from relying on the same civil rights as their neighbors. In the European states, the problem is mainly about the first and second cases: illegal migrants and legal nonnationals. In America, it is mainly about the first and the third: illegal migrants and long-resident citizens who are not treated equally. The differences in history and in law are immense, but the bottom line seems to be the same across the board. Civil rights alone are not the way to achieve equality for all. This is why, in America first and in Europe slightly later, dissatisfied citizens were forced to invent community rights.

Community rights differ from civil rights in the boundaries that they draw. It is no longer the fact of having national citizenship that matters in the struggle for equal rights. Rather, in this logic, the struggle for equality is based on a particular group identity. This identity can be based on two main criteria, ethnicity or religion. Each of these two can assume a particular political force vis-à-vis the nation-state. Both community-based calls for equal rights sound irrational at first, and they still sound irrational for many nation-state elites: What can ethnic origin or religious conviction have to do with civil equality? Yet the answer is simple, and it is underwritten also by the staunchest defenders of community-neutral civil rights (Wilson 1987). Given the long history of inequality and discrimination in every state we know, the enforcement of civil rights appears to require "affirmative action." The term, coined in America, has been translated in Europe as "reverse discrimination," "positive discrimination," or "antiracist policy." In all its variants across the West, it involves policies that require quota systems in the recruitment of employees; in the distribution of housing, schooling, and welfare services; and in the creation of promotion and career structures that put fairness in the place of past discrimination.

What affirmative action was originally expected to affirm was, quite simply, equal access to civil rights. It was to make up for the faults of history by remedial public action, taken consensually and for the common good. One could call it a logical rectification of history. What it has come to affirm, however, is not a universal faith in civil rights, but the faith of ethnic and religious communities in their right to determine their own destiny. This dialectic twist is not as surprising as it sounds: If initiatives are aimed at one or another community, that community will also be organized, mobilized, and come to be thought of as a social body with its own particular rights. In this way, affirmative action comes to affirm precisely that which civil rights were supposed to overcome: boundaries between, and a strengthened sense of identity within, ethnic or religious communities. This does not mean that one has to be against affirmative action. What it shows, however, is that the logic of civil rights and the logic of community rights, including affirmative action, are two different logics. There is no way of solving the multicultural riddle if we fudge the differences and treat one sort of rights as "bascially the same" as the other two. This conflation however, is a very fashionable fallacy. Spokespersons for the rights of religious communities appeal to their believers' faith in civil rights, spokespersons for ethnic rights translate their message into religious rights, and those who speak for a civil rights approach sell civil rights as the way toward ethnic or religious community rights. Time and again, it appears politically convenient, both for majorities and among minorities, to vacillate between the different logics. There are good reasons for this, for it makes everyone's arguments more elastic and renders compromises more flexible. At the same time, however, it can lead to the most paradoxical and counterproductive results.

The clearest examples of such a strategy of confusion are found in Europe, rather than in America, for two contradictory reasons. To start with, European states have a much longer history of ethnic or religious discrimination despite formal declarations of legal equality. Racism and communalism went on long after the formal recognition of equal civil rights for all. In America, by contrast, civil equality was denied even in principle to African Americans until 1862 (and in effect, much longer) and denied to Native Americans until 1911 (in effect, again, much longer). In most of Europe, such systematic exclusions from civil rights turned more and more unpractical in a climate of competitive industrialization. In fact, some states that oppressed their minorities lost their best entrepreneurial elites to more liberal states. One may think of the French Huguenot refugees who were outlawed for the second time in 1685, proceded to emigrate in large numbers, and soon contributed enormously to the economies of Holland and Prussia, as well as America. Conversely, however, and this is the second reason, present-day European states cannot solve their current problems of inequality by simply reinforcing civil rights because most of their ethnic and religious minorities today are recent arrivals, and thus not citizens at all.

Virtually all European states, with the main exception of Great Britain, replicate this constellation of disadvantaged minorities that do not hold national citizenship and thus civil rights. The unification of the European Community has alleviated some of these problems by encouraging member-states to treat each other's nationals like their own, regardless of the member-state from which they come. Yet these multinational legal agreements remain limited, and at any rate they do not affect the far more disadvantaged minorities that hail from beyond the European Community—Eastern Europe and the Balkans, North Africa and Turkey, Indochina and South Asia. To remedy systematic inequalities is thus again a matter of addressing and targeting these nonnationals as ethnic or religious communities, instead of as citizens. To get a feel for the resulting contradictions, it may be useful to throw a brief glance at two cases.

Probably the oldest and most odd example of fudging civil rights and religious community rights is found in the Netherlands from around 1600 to the present (van Rooden 1996). At the risk of oversimplifying four hundred years of a complicated history, I shall accentuate some key points of immediate multicultural interest. Around 1600, the Netherlands was the center of the capitalist world, with Amsterdam counting a third of world trade as its own and a third of its inhabitants as immigrants. There, the largely self-governing cities, such as Amsterdam, Utrecht, and Haarlem, faced citizenries of equal civic standing, but administered welfare rights and economic perks according to their citizens' religious communities. Some were treated better than others, but none was left entirely without a stake in the system. Even the so-called sects of Armenians and Anabaptists, as well as the Jewish community, were awarded welfare rights, and sometimes civic perks, on the basis of their religious affiliations. In the course of time (ca. 1600 to 1800), the citizens of Holland grew used to the idea that they interacted with their cities and even their state on the basis of their religious identities. This was vastly better than the oppression of religious minorities elsewhere, and it probably spurred the famous "Dutch tolerance." However, just when Holland should have started to become a modern state (ca. 1850–1900), the state-sponsored habit of religious communalism came back with a vengeance: The modernizing state was squeezed into a coma by a pincer movement between what might be called the religious right and the religious left—the Catholics, who had had a rough deal in the past, and the ultra-Protestants, who feared they might get one in the future. For the formative one hundred years of industrialization and nation-building (ca. 1850–1950), the state elite of the Netherlands was either unable or unwilling to deal with its citizens as citizens. Instead, it worked like a trust bank for three religious communities or "pillars" of national society: Catholics, so-called Orthodox Protestants, and the neither-nors who had to organize as if they, too, were a religious community. This dissolution of civil politics into a religious "pillarization" ran out of steam in the 1960s, but it has an influence on Dutch citizens' ideas about multiculturalism even now. The largest groups of nonnationals are from Turkey and from Morocco, and they have precious little in common except that both groups are Muslim. For most native Dutch, however, the problem of multiculturalism has become a problem of how to integrate or pacify

Muslims as such. The upshot is simple: It is Islam as such that most citizens now see as *the* multicultural problem and most conservatives see as a threat to Dutch values.[3]

The British example of conflating civil rights and community rights is remarkable because it is largely unnecessary. Britain is unique in Western comparison in that almost all its minority citizens are entitled to the status of nationals and thus share the same right to equal civil rights. Yet strangely and paradoxically, it is Britain that has gone furthest on the path away from a civil rights approach. While this has historical reasons,[4] it is nonetheless an astonishing example of what happens when civil rights give way to ethnic or religious rights. Britain has an institution called "The Muslim Parliament," as if Muslims were not represented at Westminster, the famed "Mother of Parliaments"; its governing Labour Party has a special "Black Section," as if there were a white and a nonwhite version of social democracy; and Britain has local authorities that involve temples and mosques in administering the naturalization of overseas migrants into British citizens (Baumann 1995b). None of these things are bad by themselves if one takes a closer look, and every country has, so far, been stuck with its own national multiculturalism, as we shall see in chapters 3 and 4. Yet what these details show is the opposite of a color-blind, culture-blind, or religion-blind—and thus secular—modern state.

To sum up, both of these European examples of putting community rights in the place of civil rights are, in their own ways, examples of affirmative action, even when they date several hundred years back. Ethnic or religious community rights are thus nothing new in modern states, but they are clearly something radically different from civil rights. It may matter little to the person whether she enjoys a right as a citizen, as an ethnically distinguishable person, or as a member of some congregation or other. A right is a right—who cares where it comes from? Yet what is right about a right? For a multiculturalist, as well as for a social scientist, there is no right in claiming a right unless it is the same right for all. It may not suit us to distinguish different kinds of rights. To solve the multicultural riddle, however, the differences are crucial, and conflating these differences will not help anyone. Yet as we have seen, this strategy of confusion is popular and politically useful. It promises everyone to have the best of all three worlds, the civic, the ethnic, and the religious; but like all political fallacies, it is most useful to those who have power already.

Throwing a more thoughtful glimpse back at King's dream, we must choose, now, who is to share this dream and in what capacity we, or they, can make it come true. Are we to share the dream as nationals regardless of color and creed, culture and ethnic identity? In that case, our solution to the multicultural riddle will require the forging of a common civil culture, but that civil culture will be a national culture, and the forging will require assimilation on the part of all, especially newcomers. Or are we to share the dream as members of our own particular ethnic community, regardless of whether we wish to be stereotyped as community people or ethnics? In that case, we risk being singled out as problem groups or as pampered minorities, and we also risk the wrath of social control as it is exercised within any community based on conformity. Are we to share the dream as members of a religious faith, regardless of who defines what we must believe in and who can rule us out as half-believers, heretics, or free-to-shoot apostates? Even if the excesses of enforcing ethnic or religious conformity were rare (and they are not!), our sole reliance on community rights would mean a state without a unifying civil culture. The choices are fundamental, because the three logics of equality are mutually exclusive. This does not mean, of course, that there is one right path and two wrong ones. What matters is, I suggest, to recognize the choices and distinguish between them, so as to translate the multicultural dream into a process of multicultural thinking. To speed up this rethinking, we need to identify the poles of power that are involved in the multicultural project. From what has been said already, there must be at least three of them, and there is a fourth, our conception of culture, that sits at the center of that triangle of powers.

Notes

1. I say "present-day" civil rights because the philosophy of civil rights in its earlier modern forms tended to turn a blind eye to differences of color as well as gender. The most lucid discussion of how we have come to think of so many desiderata in the public sphere as "rights" is given in Louis Henkin's *The Age of Rights* (1990).

2. The quote continues: "and with equal natural right, in the same manner *as if* posterity had been continued by CREATION instead of GENERATION, . . . and consequently every child born into the world *must be considered* as deriving its existence from God. [Because] the world is as new to him as it was to the first man that existed, and his natural right is of the same kind" (Conway 1967, 304–05; capitals in original; italics mine). In other words, Paine argues, all religions view every child as a creation by God, rather than a creation by sex ("generation"), because it knows as little about the world as did the first human being created by God. We know of no such society, but the trick is well played by putting words like "consequently" and "as if" in the wrong places.

3. This development is further encouraged by the fact that the term "Muslim" can function as a code word to distinguish the more recent immigrants of Mediterranean origins from those who originate from the former Dutch colonies of Suriname and Indonesia. Although the latter comprise many Muslims, too, it is the former who are usually talked of as "the Muslim immigrants." To call them after their religion may serve to scale down a prevailing feeling that they are more distant from Dutch ways than the former colonials, and it may thus lower the odds in any situation of conflict. I owe these observations to Alex Strating.

4. Among these historical reasons are the absence of both a written constitution and a bill of civil rights. The paradox also becomes more understandable as soon as one realizes the difference between nationality and citizenship. The British state, inheritor to an unmanageably populous Empire, proceeded to institute five different kinds of citizenship, each with its own package of civil rights. The American state has done likewise by inventing different kinds of citizenship for different categories of citizens, mainly depending on their countries of origin. For defenders of a unified civil rights approach, it must be imperative to counteract such hierarchies of citizenship. I owe these remarks to Marie-Benedicte Dembour.

Further Reading

Dembour, Marie-Benedicte. 1996. "Human Rights Talk and Anthropological Ambivalence: The Particular Contexts of Universal Claims." Pp. 18–39 in *Inside and Outside the Law*, ed. O. Harris. London: Routledge.

2

From Dreaming to Meaning:
The Multicultural Triangle

National Culture, Ethnic Culture, Religion as Culture

A philosopher was asked what the Earth rested on.
"A tortoise," said the philosopher.
"And what does the tortoise rest on?"
"A table."
"And what does the table rest on?"
"An elephant."
"And what does the elephant rest on?"
"Don't be inquisitive." (H. D. F. Kitto 1951, 176)

The method we adopt . . . consists of the following operations:

i. define the phenomenon under study as a relation between two or more terms, real or supposed;

ii. construct a table of possible permutations between these terms;

iii. take this table as the general object of analysis which, at this level only, can yield necessary connections, [with] the empirical phenomenon considered at the beginning being only one possible combination among others. (Levi-Strauss 1964, 16)

The Multicultural Riddle

THE FIRST CORNER of the multicultural triangle is the state, in particular, the so-called modern state or Western nation-state. It is the governing elite of the state, as well as its hegemonic media and its dominant civil culture, that determine the life chances of most people, be they counted as majorities or minorities through one criteria or another. It is precisely these powers, in fact, that often determine who is regarded as a minority and on what construction of difference, be it ethnic or religious, civic or sexual, historic or mythical. Although the choice of this starting point may seem obvious, it is nonetheless useful to cast a very brief glance behind the facade of this entity. The Western nation-state is a peculiar amalgam of two seemingly irreconcilable philosophies: rationalism, that is, the appeal to purpose and efficiency; and romanticism, that is, the appeal to feelings as the basis of action.

On the one hand, the modern nation-state grew out of the economic and geopolitical necessities of early modern Europe. From around 1400, Europeans faced expanding populations with non-expanding production technologies. To relieve their population pressure and acreage limitations, they tried territorial warfare for the first few hundred years. Within Europe, this was a zero-sum game: The continent grew no bigger, and all available resources were wasted in an endless succession of mutual wars. The second strategy was colonizing the lands overseas, and it paid the bills for about two hundred more years. Yet even this escape route came to an end. Both World War I (1914–1918) and even World War II (1939–1945) can be seen as European powers fighting amongst themselves about the rest of the world. American governments, who had a different vision of colonialism, managed to dismantle the old European-owned empires within fifteen years (ca. 1945–1960) and substituted a new free-trade imperialism, or "Coca-Cola globalization," in its place. What happened in between, however, was a new cult of the Western-style nation-state as the ultimate entity to shape the world. This cult is known as the doctrine of sovereignty, the foundation myth of every state since then and until now. Nation-state sovereignty is the doctrine of advancing economic expansion by establishing a territorial monopoly on the legitimate use of physical force. It is the state alone that launches wars and draws peace treaties, controls police forces and prisons, and regulates when a citizen may carry arms. By using this monopoly on force to protect, control, and expand economic activity, the state could function, or be seen to function in due time, as the most rational provider of public welfare (de Swaan 1988).

On the other hand, another source of the modern West arises from a romantic vision of ethnicity as the basis of state making and nation building. The wellsprings of this romanticism reach back to the eighteenth century and are often tagged with the name of the philosopher Herder, whom we will meet later. The idea is simple enough: The world is populated by peoples, and each of these has its culture. The final expression of this cultural unity is the making of a state, an act that promotes the cultural or ethnic group to the status, some say liberty, of a nation. The simplicity of this view is seductive, and we will come back to it to dismantle its dangerous errors.

The second pole of multiculturalism is the idea that ethnicity is the same as cultural identity. The idea of ethnicity has one great advantage over that of "the state": No one needs abstract thinking to know what it is. It is roots—where I come from, what makes me who I am, in one phrase, natural identity. Or so it seems. Familiar as these intuitions are, they take a serious battering in rethinking the multicultural dream. Ethnic absolutism is neither politically useful nor even tenable as an analysis. Even social scientists, who are not known for their radicalism, have been dismantling it for nearly fifty years.[1] What, then, is wrong with ethnicity as one's only identity, or ethnic identity as an absolute?

Taken at face value, the idea of ethnicity appeals, first and foremost, to blood from the past. It invokes biological ancestry and then claims that present-day identities follow from this ancestry. This may be true in the breeding of dogs, but it cannot be applied to human beings. Of the many fallacies it entails, I shall only mention four. First, descent, that is, the tracing of persons from ancestors, is an act of present-day memory looking back, as opposed to an authentic act of genealogical bookkeeping. Even people such as the Nuer, who depend on descent for their whole social order, revise their genealogical memories and adjust them to changing needs (Evans-Pritchard 1940, 1951). Second, even a scientifically ascertained individual ancestry does not determine patterns of behavior or preferences among humans. Genetics may influence our looks and even our horizons, but these can come to be transformed in the light of individual choices and experience: Compare the faces or bodies of any pair of twins who choose separate careers or role models to follow. The case is even stronger with regard to behavior: One is not simply born to act or feel as one does. Rather, what decides one's life are the actions and attitudes one takes vis-à-vis the culture, or cultures, that one identifies as one's own. It is thus a matter of perception and will mediated by culture, or of culture mediated by perception and will.

Third, and on the collective scale, even the most racist biologists have failed, despite generous funding from eugenicists in America and fascists in Europe, to establish any link whatsoever between race or ethnicity and mental properties, behaviors, or even preferences for behaviors. The term "race" itself is a fallacious nineteenth-century fiction, and the term "ethnicity" in its presumed biological sense is its late-twentieth-century photocopy. Its outlines are vaguer, but the design of the picture is just as bad. Even if human behavior was determined by genetics, which it is not, the genetic differences among humans are far too small to account for the cultural differences we know. The total genetic variety across the human species affects no more than 4 percent of the gene pool we share, and while they affect physical looks, they have no mental, let alone cultural, significance. What the biologist can observe in studying these limited variations are not boundaries between "races," but rather "clines" of distribution. "Clines" is the term introduced by Livingstone and Dobzhansky (1962) to decribe how each of the different genetic factors shows its own statistical peaks across the entire continuum of the human population. Since the peaks do not fall into heaps, but rather cut across each other at random points across the whole spectrum, they clearly show "the non-existence of human races" (p. 279).

Finally, just as people emphasize different aspects of their language, body language, behavior, and style in different situations, so too do they emphasize or abjure the attributes of their ethnicity. In social science code, we therefore speak of "shifting identity" or "contextual ethnicity." Ethnic identities are thus nothing more than acts of ethnic identification that are frozen in time. As the social climate gets colder, they can go into deepfreeze and harden; as the social climate gets warmer, they can unfreeze and melt into new forms. Analytically speaking, ethnicity is not an identity given by nature, but an identification created through social action. We shall return to this point in chapter 5.

The third corner of the multicultural triangle is religion for two reasons. Religion can sound absolute, and it can serve as a translation for all other manner of perceived group conflict. Let us briefly examine these two reasons, for they are not as clear-cut as they seem. Religion can sound absolute, that is, it can be made to sound as if it determines objective and unchangeable differences between people. These are often thought to be basic and cast in stone by powers above human will and human history. Religions are, after all, concerned with the seemingly absolute matters of life and death, good and evil, merit and failure—in other words, the meaning and morality of life. There is no doubt that most believers think that this is true, and a social science of religion needs to recognize this fact. It does, after all, motivate believers to the actions that we need to understand. At the same time, however, it would be naive for a social scientist to take on board the absolute claims of one religion, another religion, or even all religions. The very idea of calling some things religious, and other things not, is a result of very particular historical processes. This has been shown most forcefully by Talal Asad (1993a), an expert on both Islam and Christianity, who concluded that "there cannot be a universal definition of religion . . . because that definition is itself the historical product of discursive processes" (p. 29). These discursive processes were not forged in some historical or political no man's land, but answered to very tangible conflicts about the distribution of power, authority, and legitimacy. Even today, Asad finds, the separation of what counts as religion from what counts as politics answers to very particular vested interests. Interestingly, these interests connect parties that otherwise find it hard to agree:

> [T]his effort of defining religion converges with the liberal demand in our time that it be kept quite separate from politics, law, and science—spaces in which varieties of power and reason articulate our distinctively modern life. This definition is at once part of a strategy (for secular liberals) of the confinement, and (for liberal Christians) of the defense of religion. Yet this separation of religion from power is a modern Western norm, the product of a unique post-Reformation history. (Asad 1993a, 28)

Other authors have confirmed the peculiar history of these consciously "modern" distinctions between "religion" as such and "politics" as such (Harrison 1990). These distinctions are ideological and cannot be taken at face value as if they were "pure" analytical distinctions. This is no less true of Islam than of Christianity: "The attempt to understand Muslim traditions by insisting that in them religion and politics (two essences modern society tries to keep conceptually and practically apart) are coupled must, in my view, lead to failure" (Asad 1993a, 28). What is at stake here is an essentialized idea of religion, and we will come back to it in chapter 6 when we discuss its dangers for the multicultural project. Any theory of multiculturalism must beware of the misunderstanding that religion is a class of facts different from other social facts. The boundaries between religion and the rest of the social world are blurred, and they answer to political, ideological, and even academic ambitions. Even within these boundaries, furthermore, religions show an enormous range of flexibility and change, as we will see.

Nonetheless, religion faces us with the semblance of absolute dividing lines, and most people take these for granted throughout their lives. This is not a matter of academic training, let alone a lack of it: If I may speak personally, I do it myself. Although I believe in no god, I still call myself "culturally, a Catholic." Perhaps this kind of mechanism is one more reason for the second paradox about religion in the multicultural triangle: Precisely because religion sounds so absolute, it can be used as a translation for other, more relative, forms of conflict. In complex situations of social strife, one can often find ethnic, national, or migratory boundaries transformed into religious ones. I have already touched on one recent example of such a transformation: In the Netherlands, the native Dutch first perceived an influx of national minorities such as Turks and Moroccans, yet they proceeded to translate this national minority problem into a religious minority problem concerned with Muslims and Islam. Another example may be taken from the United States: While mainstream opinion identifies ethnicity as the root cause of inequality between black and white Americans, African American Muslims translate the conflict into one between a liberating Islam and an oppressive Christianity. There are many more examples—from the conquest of Latin America to the so-called "religious wars" of early modern Europe and from the former Yugoslavia to present-day Northern Ireland—of people redefining a conflict between national or ethnic interests and identities into a so-called "war of religions." The consequences of this translation have one thing in common: They block the way back to political or even multicultural dialogue, for what can look more religious than blood that is sacrificed to the seemingly "absolute" dividing line of religion? Categorizing an event as a "religious conflict" is always effective in raising the stakes in whatever confrontation people find themselves.

Having pinpointed the three corners of the multicultural triangle, we can now see what is hidden at its center. It is, I suggest, the magnet of culture. What is at stake in all debates about nation making, ethnicity, and religious difference is invariably the idea of culture and what it is taken, by the different contenders in the multicultural debate, to signify. At the risk of oversimplifying matters at this rethinking stage, we can distinguish two ideas of culture that have made their way into the social sciences. As we will see, only one of these has made headway among the three parties in the multicultural debate, that is, the defenders of building national cultures, the protagonists of ethnic cultures, and those who view religion as culture.

The first view of culture, which may be called the essentialist, is by far the most widespread. Its history and philosophy are traced to Gottfried Herder and his contemporaries around 1800. These were cosmopolitan thinkers who wanted to validate every "people" and "race" in terms of their own traditions and cultural productions. They thus collected everything "ethnic," from age-old myths to everyday recipes for baking blueberry pies, and helped to put every culture into the record of human history. This respect for folk traditions, hitherto despised by the educated elite, made its way into the social sciences. Here, it was championed by Franz Boas, the founder of anthropology in America. Boas, who had to escape his native Germany because of anti-Jewish intolerance, had read Herder in his youth and applied this new respect for native traditions in his studies of Native Americans. His influence continues to shape American anthropology even now, one hundred years after his career reached its height. The view of culture that was first invented by Herder and then perfected by Boas is still important today. It comprehends culture as the collective heritage of a group, that is, as a catalog of ideas and practices that shape both the collective and the individual lives and thoughts of all members. Culture thus appears as a mold that shapes lives or, to put it somewhat polemically, as a giant photocopy machine that keeps turning out identical copies. This view is plausible in some ways and ludicrous in others.

For the plausibility of the essentialist view of culture, one need only ask parents or children, no matter where, what the word culture means to them. It is perceived as a heritage with rules and norms that fixes the difference both between right and wrong and between Us and Them. To socialize a child is always also to enculturate the child, to tell him or her that "this is what We do, so do it; and that is what They do, so don't!" And no one will deny that every cultural collective shows a certain stability in the traits and tastes, styles and routines that its participants have learned to cultivate. The essentialist view of culture is thus not without its plausibility; we get a fairly clear picture when we speak of national cultures such as German or British, as well as when we speak of religious cultures, such as Catholic or, with Max Weber (1930), the spirit of Protestantism. This concept of essentialized culture is a key item in the armory of all three parties that debate the multicultural riddle.

Yet the plausibility of this view goes only so far. One need only apply the chicken-and-egg question to ask: Who is it that cultivates culture? True, culture maketh man, but it is men, women, and youths who make culture. If they ceased to make it and remake it, culture would cease to be; and all making of culture, no matter how conservative, is also a remaking. Even at its most conservative, it places old habits in new contexts, and it thus changes the significance of these habits. Just as often, people change and adjust, fine-tune and rework the habits themselves. One need not go far to find endless examples: In the space of twenty years, every single culture changes its ways of speaking, celebrating birthdays or community occasions, treating students or the unemployed, going through childbirth or funerals, dealing with nature or space, and even viewing their culture in the abstract. If culture is not the same as cultural change, then it is nothing at all.

Culture in this second understanding, which may be called the processual, is not so much a photocopy machine as a concert, or indeed a historically improvised jam session. It only exists in the act of being performed, and it can never stand still or repeat itself without changing its meaning. This processual view has found its way into the social sciences, especially where they rely on intensive fieldwork and the practices of participant observation (Borofsky 1995). It is equally evident in quantitative methods such as questionnaires that tell us of, say, changing food tastes among the French or changing views on contraception among Catholics. In doing empirical research, whether on multiculturalism or anything else, the photocopy view of culture must always be represented: After all, it is the more widespread, and informants will volunteer it most readily. Yet it is represented not as a truth, but as one of the things that our informants, or the people we corepresent, believe and enact. It forms part of the multicultural riddle that we need to solve, but it is not the solution of that riddle. We shall try to do justice to both views in chapter 7.

With the multicultural triangle thus laid out and its enigmatic center pencilled in, it is possible now to examine in more detail the first pole of power, the nation-state. We can uncover two problems: (1) Nation-state and ethnicity stand in a peculiar relation to each other because of the romantic heritage of the nation concept; and (2) nation-state and religion stand in a tense relation because of the rationalist and secularist traditions of the modern state. Let us take each problem in turn over the next two chapters.

Notes

1. Some of this work is discussed in chapter 5. The best summary and the most interesting updates of these fifty years of work are presented in three exhaustive surveys of the vast anthropological literature: *Ethnicity and Nationalism* by Thomas Eriksen (1993); *Ethnicity: Anthropological Constructions* by Marcus Banks (1996); and *Rethinking Ethnicity* by Richard Jenkins (1997). Excerpts from many of the classic contributions are reprinted in: *Ethnicity*, edited by Hutchinson and Smith (1996). Readers who wish not to dive too deep into this sea of scholarship are best served by reading Jenkins (1994), which addresses most of the salient questions.

Further Reading

Asad, Talal. 1993a. "Anthropological Conceptions of Religion: Reflections on Geertz." Pp. 27–54 in *Genealogies of Religion: Discipline and Reasons of Power in Christianity and Islam*, ed. T. Asad. Baltimore: Johns Hopkins University Press.

Jenkins, Richard. 1994. "Rethinking Ethnicity: Identity, Categorization, and Power." *Ethnic and Racial Studies* 17: 197–223.

3

The Nation-State, I:
Postethnic or Pseudotribe?

Why Nation-States Are Not
Ethnically Neutral

The mind of this city [-state of Athens] is so noble and free and so powerful and healthy . . . because we are pure Hellenes and not commingled with barbarians. (Menexos, according to Plato [ca. 380 BCE], cited in Connor 1993, 386)

Providence has been pleased to give this one connected country [the United States] to one united people—a people descended from the same ancestors. (John Jay, 1787, in Hamilton et al. 1937, 9, cited in Connor 1993, 380)

We have the same ancestors, we are of the same family, we are all brothers and sisters. . . . No one can divide the children of the same family. Likewise, no one can divide Viet-Nam. (Ho Chi Minh 1967, 158, cited in Connor 1993, 379)

Our answer, then, to that often asked question, "What is a nation?" is that it is a group of people who feel that they are ancestrally related. (Connor 1993, 382)

The Multicultural Riddle

THE HYPHENATED HYBRID "nation-state" combines nation, a reassuring and warmly emotional idea, with the rather distant and cold-sounding reality of the state. This sweet-and-sour mix can serve as one of the delicacies of the historical and linguistic imagination. Let us see in detail how it has been cooked up.

In using the word "state" in modern times, we mean a form of governance that is centralized, holds or claims territorial sovereignty, holds or claims a monopoly on coercive force in that territory, and works on a system of membership based on individual citizenship. This form is a latecomer in human history, and it is only over the past one hundred years that every bit of the globe has been claimed by one state or another, sometimes two. States are the things we pay taxes to, pledge allegiance to, accept laws from, and get passports or visas to enter—all because they claim a territorial monopoly on coercive force. Nationality, which is recognized or denied by each state on its own rules, entitles a person to a passport; this passport can, although it need not, entitle the person to citizenship, but this citizenship is always selective: Not everyone may have it. The rest is legal argument. What, however, is a nation-state; or, what is a nation?

A nation is one or several ethnic groups whose members think, or are thought in some way, to "own" a state, that is, to carry a special responsibility for it. In case this sounds surprisingly simple, let us compare what the two words, ethnic group or tribe on the one hand and nation on the other, are found to mean in different languages. The table below is based on a comparison of dictionary definitions in twelve languages, which include Indo-European languages such as English, French, German, Spanish, Russian, and others, and Arabic and Chinese. As the table shows, the same set of criteria is used to define what the two concepts mean.

The Nation-State, I: Postethnic or Pseudotribe?

Dictionary Definitions of "Ethnic Group" and "Nation"

Ethnic Group	Nation
Based on descent	Based on descent
Often recognizable by looks	Often recognizable by looks
Sharing cultural traits (language, outlook, etc.)	Sharing cultural traits (language, outlook, etc.)
Said to be acquired from birth	Said to be acquired from birth
Forming a community of destiny and some form of political organization	Forming a community of destiny on the basis of a state

Not every dictionary lists all characteristics for both concepts: in American, English, and German dictionaries, for instance, nationality is not thought to be "recognizable by looks," and the idea of a "community of destiny" is more common in the Latin languages such as French and Spanish than in the Germanic ones such as Dutch and Swedish. Yet every dictionary consulted lists at least five of the criteria, and the lists run in parallel except for the criteria of political or state organization. The homology is striking, but the explanation is simple. Since modern nation-states arose in the West, roughly from 1500 AD onward, they had to overcome the boundaries of ethnicity among their citizens, and they did so by turning the nation into a superethnos. The nation is thus both postethnic, in that it denies the salience of old ethnic distinctions and portrays these as a matter of a dim and distant prestate past, and superethnic, in that it portrays the nation as a new and bigger kind of ethnos. Most nation-states, however, have failed to complete this project in that they included some ethnic groups and excluded others, or privileged some and marginalized others. It is precisely this exclusion that turns numbers of people into "minorities" and thereby creates the key problem between the nation-state and the multicultural project. Every nation-state has one superethnos, called *the* Germans, *the* French, or *the* American people, whose members think they have founded it or should have a special role in running it. To be truly postethnic, that is, truly inclusive, the nation-state would have to cease constructing its nation as a superethnos. A multicultural nation-state is, in some ways, a contradiction in terms.

Yet like all conclusions from logic, this sounds more gloomy than it really is. True, no state is perfect, and real multiculturalism would have to be global—just as environmentalism and feminism need to be global to succeed. It is equally true, however, that every Western nation-state has made some headway, over the past twenty years, in encouraging a multicultural culture. How could they succeed in this when certain ethnic groups were excluded or marginalized in every nation-state we know? There are probably two answers to this. One is welfare, the other is mystique. The first is economic and is based upon the rationalist philosophy of the modern state. The second is ideological and is based on the romantic roots of the nation-state.

By the first answer, loosely called welfare, I mean the achievement of Western states to keep most people from starving. Let us not ask at this stage at which other states' expense this First World achievement has been gained and sustained. The nation-state in the West has been able, despite the official end of colonialism and the real end of full employment, to house and feed almost all, or all that had a political voice. This was not so much an act of charity as an act of self-preservation. The world order of nation-states would have collapsed long ago had not state elites bought off the poor and the minorities—conveniently, often the same people. State elites have had considerable success, in the West, in portraying the nation-state as a postethnic megastore that exists to serve everyone's economic needs, regardless of color, culture, or creed. If the West were poor, ethnic conflicts would certainly be far more bloody than they are;

there is plenty of evidence all around us that poverty and increased competition for scarce resources increase intra-ethnic solidarities and cross-ethnic tensions. If ethnic belonging becomes a resource in economic competition, then ethnic radicalization is an all but inevitable consequence. The nation-state of the West has invested all its multicultural credentials into projecting itself as the greatest shopping mall of all, a selfless postethnic provider of economic services for everyone. It portrays itself, often convincingly, as a value-free dispenser of well-being and justice regardless of culture, that is, as a kind of postethnic bargain basement.

Individual citizens may believe this or not, and even whole communities of citizens may cast doubt on the postethnic welfare achievement of the state. Yet the recourse to legally enforceable civil rights has been improved almost everywhere. State elites have improved upon their past records of racism or systematic negligence, and most citizens can now hope, or successfully fight, for equal rights of access to state welfare provisions. This is a strong argument for the postethnic character of the Western nation-state. That said, however, we face a historical paradox, or at least a bill that neither the state, nor the rich, are prepared to pay.

Western nation-state elites wish to promise social security for all alike. They compete on this promise on party lines, and no party is happy to lose. Yet there is still no such thing as a free lunch. Nation-state elites need to motivate the people they wish to govern so that their citizens remain prepared to chip in their share of taxes for the greater good and, if need be, surrender their private moral scruples for the greater national glory. All this is done, not in the name of the state as such, let alone of its governing elites. Nor is it done in the name of any one of the privileged ethnic groups. Rather, it is at this point of moral commitment and community building that the idea of nation comes into its own. In appealing to national consciousness and conscience, the state can be portrayed as the servant, not of the privileged ethnic groups within it, but of the all-inclusive megaethnicity called nation. It thus creates its own mystique of a new and all-inclusive postethnic community.

Strangely, of the two ancestries of the Western nation-state, the rationalist and the romantic, one is rather more alive in America, the other one in Europe. This sounds straightforward, but there is an ironic historical twist in this development, for these two parts of the West have exchanged places vis-à-vis the rationalist or romanticist ideology of the state. Romantic folk nationalism has its deepest roots in Europe, but it is the European states that have gone furthest in disowning their ethno-nationalist heritage. Most Europeans, whether native citizens or immigrants, want the state as a value-free provider of economic services and, please, nothing else. With the sole exception of neofascist splinter groups among the politically retarded, the symbols, rituals, and even the language of ethno-national patriotism have all but vanished from both the public and even the private spheres. It is among Americans, the nonethnic nation if ever there was one, that we now find the romantic heritage of "one-blood" patriotism in its clearest form. Faced with this paradox, one of my American students even came up with an ethno-national answer: "We're all mongrels," he said, "with a quarter-ethnic identity from here and a quarter from there: So since everyone is mixed, we can be all the same." I do not expect all readers to agree with this view, but its dialectic logic is fascinating nevertheless: It is the multiethnic hybridity of many American citizens that is used to argue for a shared neoethnic endorsement of national unity. If everyone's ancestry were "mixed," then everyone's present identity would be the same: superethnically American.

Looking for other explanations for this cross-Atlantic shift in the understanding of the nation-state, one would probably turn to historical processes. By the time that Europeans invented their various versions of ethno-nationalism, mostly in the nineteenth century, they had already experienced several centuries of state-run centralized bureaucracies. These bureaucracies aimed at economic growth for each territorial state, and they tried to organize the distribution of the accruing wealth to protect their own position and prevent revolts and revolutions. They thus concentrated all political and economic power in the hands of absolute rulers. As industrialization made the poor even poorer and turned landless peasants into jobless proletarians, the system exploded in two ways at the same time. Politically, the absolute sovereignty of monarchs was replaced by the absolute sovereignty of "the people"—or whoever was recognized as such. Economically, the movements of trade unionists and socialists demanded and forced that the old bureaucratic structures must now actively redistribute the profits from industrial growth. In the course of one hundred years, roughly speaking from 1848 to 1948, all European states became welfare states, that is, states in which the governing elites are held responsible for redistributing economic profits from the richer to the poorer (de Swaan 1988). In this history, the invention of ethno-nationalism had no chance of succeeding in the long term. It managed to turn territorial states into nation-states and to turn nationalists into colonialists. But it exploded in the Europeans' face when it unleashed World War I and, on the basis of the renewed ethno-nationalism of fascism, World War II. Since then, all European nationals have learned, in their own particular ways, that nation-states had little to gain from romantic ethno-nationalism. The strength of bureaucratic, centralized, and socialist traditions throughout Europe was harnessed, from about 1960, to serve the project of a European Union. What remnants of ethno-nationalism have been reawakened in Europe can only be understood as a protest against this project of a Europe beyond nations, historically insensitive and bureaucratically heavy-handed as it may be.

The Multicultural Riddle

In America, the trend has run the other way around. Here, there was no ethnic basis to create "one American people." What made America grow into a unified state were vastly divergent regional histories of settlement and conquest, ethnocide and slavery, and, latterly, an unequal but also unbridled competition for economic self-gratification. Comparing it to European states, the United States shows none of the three factors that led Europeans to forge their nation-state unities: a tradition of the state redistributing economic gains, a strong socialist or social welfare tradition, and, less luckily, a great public tolerance of centralized state bureaucracies. Thus, forging an American national identity had to depend upon forging an explicitly post-ethnic national consciousness. How could this be done?

To understand the postethnic mystique of the modern state, it is best to consult the work of Benedict Anderson (1983), a historian at Cornell. What Anderson showed in his book, albeit between the lines, was as simple as it was revealing: Our modern idea of nationhood is a metaphysical concept. It owes its success to succeeding two even more irrational constructs. One of these is the faith in the legitimacy of power that used to be provided by dynasties, such as the Hapsburgs in multiethnic (although racist) Austria or the Ming in multiethnic (although racist) China. On the face of it, it is hard to imagine how the accident of birth could possibly count as a passport to legitimate power. But people believed in it then, and in some ways they believe in it even now. Witness First Lady widows elected to succeed their husbands in Argentina and the Philippines, Bangladesh, and Sri Lanka; witness the Kennedys, the Gandhis, the Bhuttos, not to mention all those lesser dynasties that "only" make it to heading a central bank or a media empire for three or four generations. Even the fictional dynasties that we learn to trace in soap operas and romantic novels keep showing us that money is nothing without the legitimacy of descent. It is thus perfectly understandable, if not altogether "rational" to common sense, that people might believe in dynastic succession as a ticket to legitimate rule.

The second principle of legitimizing power that Anderson (1983) saw to have been replaced by a new nationalist legitimation was, less surprisingly, the power of the churches. As normal people's lives grew more and more intertwined with the designs of state elites and their secularist programs of progress, the common people saw less and less promise in bending their knees. Instead, they bent their backs to work for a better living and send their children to school. These were run by state elites for the rich, by churches for the poor. Schooling promised chances that most parents had never had, and when farmers' children flocked to industrial cities, mass urbanization made these chances a must. At the same time, however, the state took over the schools. The school became the school of the nation, in many ways the mission station of national consciousness. It is an arresting contrast to compare literacy training for the young as this transition took place. As long as the churches ran popular schooling, the aim was to read the Bible. In eighteenth-century Sweden, then the country with the highest literacy rate in the world, no one was allowed to be married unless they could read, or pretend to read, the holy book (Johansson 1981). As soon as the nation-states took over universal schooling, the curricula were enriched with the new sacred legends of national glory. These could be ancient kings or the Declaration of Independence, great colonial victories or little stories of heroic resistance: In all cases, no matter where, the curriculum became a tool to forge a superethnic, and often newly religious, national consciousness. The philosopher Ernest Gellner, who wrote an influential book on nationalism (1983), recognized this well: The nation-state would be nothing, nowadays, if it had not taken possession of the schools. Yet he also made a strange mistake, claiming that nationalism was the end of all religious sensitivities. What happened was quite the opposite.

Each nation-state invented its own national branch of a world-wide new religion. It was called nationalism, that is, the faith that one's own moral self is inseparably bound up with one's national identity. We shall examine this strange process in the next chapter. For the moment, however, we may cast a smiling sideways glance at how nationalism has shaped even the languages themselves with which we try to go beyond a nationalist view of the world. The takeover of education by the state changed not only the content of what was learned but also the language in which it was thought. Nation-state schools turned mother tongues—untidy, regional, and often cross-border as they were—into national languages, standardized and state-bounded as they now are. An early example comes from the French Academy, founded in 1635 as a state-appointed language watchdog; the funniest comes from the United States, where some nineteenth-century Congressmen resolved that (1) an independent nation needed an independent language, and (2) one must therefore spell "labor" for labour and "center" for centre if one wants to be a good American.

Nationalism, a term by which Anderson means nothing worse than a person's faith in the moral duties incumbent on citizenship, became a substitute religion. What made it fit to act as such was that it shared one peculiar trick with its two predecessors: It could lead people to imagine themselves in community with people they did not know, or possibly even want to know, in daily life. What Anderson's book has diagnosed is thus an astonishing process. People used to think of themselves as members of a community held together by a dynastic authority, or people used to think of themselves as members of a community of faith. Through the intervention of mother tongue literacy, mass media, and state elites, people began to conceive of themselves as members of a new imagined community—the nation and its state. The nation is imagined as a community in the sense that membership confers and demands a universal bond of solidarity or, in its typically patriarchal language, brotherhood. This solidarity is imagined in that it encompasses far more people than any individual will ever know or meet. Yet it is nonetheless real for that; witness only the acts of self-sacrifice, as well as the basest beastialities, that people are prepared to commit in the name of their nation. National consciousness is thus saturated with values and ultimate identifications—just like a religion.

Unfortunately, Anderson does not show the historical processes by which these identifications took hold, but he pinpoints two of the key mechanisms that were involved. They have even given rise to a new word, "print capitalism," that is, the combination of a national language print culture with an expansive capitalist economy. What is further most useful of Anderson's analysis is the following observation (1983, chap. 8): Since the greatest majority of people do not choose their nationality, national identity tends to appear to them as a matter of ancestry and birth, an attribute that feels as natural as kinship and family do. We have seen earlier, in chapter 2, that the purportedly biological character of ancestry, kinship, and descent are popular fictions. But this does not detract from their social efficacy.

In exploring more deeply the social efficacy of nationalism or national consciousness, we are thus faced with an utterly artificial construction. It is artificial, as opposed to natural, in that it represents an ingenious artifice of the human and social imagination. What is imagined is a community that is ethnic in its history, postethnic in its civil rights and material rights standards, and superethnic to justify its existence for and as a nation. This superethnic character, however, takes on mystical and almost religious traits. Nationalism, the ideology of one or a few privileged ethnic categories within a state, still disadvantages other ethnic categories in the same state. Even when discrimination is abolished in law, it carries on in daily practice. These are the ethnic categories that state bureaucracies stylize into "groups" and then call, or rather turn into, minorities. Yet the nation-state has not faltered on these failings. How, then, can such a construction be plausible, and how can it motivate actions that people would be too prudent, too cowardly, and sometimes even too decent to commit for their own sakes? The answer must lie in a combination of politico-economic power and national symbolic persuasiveness. Let us see how this works, and how each state has been provided with its own national religion or quasi-religious nationalism.

Further Reading

Anderson, Benedict. 1991. *Imagined Communities: Reflections on the Origin and Spread of Nationalism*. London: Verso; esp. pp. 14–40, 41–65.

Connor, Walker. 1993. "Beyond Reason: The Nature of the Ethnonational Bond." *Ethnic and Racial Studies* 16 (3): 373–89.

4

The Nation-State, II:
Business or Temple?

Why Nation-States Are Not Religiously Neutral

And did those feet in ancient time
walk upon England's mountains green?
And was the Holy Lamb of God
on England's pleasant pastures seen?

And did the Countenance Divine
shine forth upon our clouded hills?
And was Jerusalem builded here
among these dark satanic mills?

Bring me my bow of burning gold!
Bring me my arrows of desire!
Bring me my spear! O clouds unfold!
Bring me my chariot of fire!

I will not cease from mental fight,
nor shall my sword sleep in my hand:
Till we have built Jerusalem
in England's green and pleasant land.

> (William Blake 1808: preface to *Milton: A Poem
> in Two Books* [London: Robert Hartley Cromek])

The Multicultural Riddle

OF THE DOZEN or so occasions when I have seen adult Brits cry in front of strangers, this song accounts for four. Sung to one of the finest hymn tunes ever written,[1] it encapsulates the dream of turning early industrial England, with its satanically inhuman factory mills, into a free Jerusalem for all. The feet that Blake mentions are those of Jesus, whom medieval folk traditions believed to have journeyed across England, and the new Jerusalem is a state of justice and equality, a kind of Christian socialism pioneered in one country. There are several parallels, both in Europe and the United States, of likening the nation to the original Chosen People who were promised Jerusalem, that is, the achievement of a divinely just social order on earth. The thought is not as mad as it looks.

When using the rationalist language of costs and benefits, state elites tell their citizens that they provide the best value for money. Pay your taxes, obey our laws, and you will get the best deal available anywhere. When this rationalist language will not do, state elites need to fall back on something more noble, and what can be nobler than a faith that binds all citizens? As we have seen already in designing the multicultural triangle, religion, with its claims to ultimate truths and its potential social divisiveness, is the oldest problem of the nation-state. What better idea, therefore, than establishing a quasi religion for all citizens?

The first and still the most exciting reconnaissance of such a civil religion was written by the eminently [sic] American political scientist Robert Bellah (1966). This was a short article only, but it was written at a crucial time. Trying to square his American values with the values of his government practicing genocide on the Vietnamese, he asked the question: Who are we, and what makes us tick? He discovered something astonishing, and he even added a few pages at the end to apply his discovery so as not to seem unpatriotic. His discovery, which he labeled correctly at once, has remained known ever since as Civil

The Nation-State, II: Business or Temple?

Religion. On the one hand, and as shown by Anderson (1983), the nation-state and its secularizing nationalist ideology were supposed to be the successors of religious community feeling. On the other hand, Bellah's seminal paper can still serve best to show how nationalism can take on the mantle of religion even in the most consciously modern of nation-states.[2]

Everyone is used to hearing churchy-sounding blessings at the end of political speeches: "God bless America; God bless you all." This might sound like mere ritual, but then again, ritual is the classic place where people give themselves away: Their rituals make clear what all their purposive behaviors try to hide. So it is worth looking at rituals twice, and what Bellah came up with was shocking. American civil culture, the least church-ridden of all, was replete with religious-sounding references and rituals.

This seemingly secular state views itself as a "Nation under God," whose constitution stresses its "duty before God" to ensure, in turn, the "rights of man [that] come from the hands of God," much as Tom Paine put it first. Its commonest means of social exchange, the dollar bill, bears three religious inscriptions and symbols, and its geography is dotted with sacred national places: Liberty Hall, the Lincoln Memorial, the Gettysburg National Cemetery, Arlington, Mount Rushmore, and others. The seasonal cycle of all its citizens is ordered by sacred national feasts: Independence Day celebrates the fusion of all ethnic groups into "one nation under God" (Washington); Thanksgiving Day celebrates the American family and its descent from the, officially, peaceful settlers of New England; Memorial Day celebrates all those who "gave their lives so that the nation may live" (Lincoln), and the ultimate saint of Memorial Day is, quite tellingly, the Unknown Soldier: a bloke from next door. Bellah's article does not mention Labor Day, but this ritual, too, which European states celebrate on May 1, is a celebration of a religio-national brotherhood: Just as Memorial Day celebrates the unknown soldiers shot dead, so labor days celebrate the unknown workers, the low-paid who create "the wealth of the nation." Also too late for Bellah's article came the latest update of the soldierly hero cult: the religious mystique that now surrounds the first "body bag" sent "home" from a foreign military intervention. This is an interesting development: War heroes are now seen as war victims, and this may even jeopardize popular support for the state using its military arm, yet the nation-state is as eager as ever to surround the political use of soldiers' lives with a state-sponsored religious mystique.

For all this and more, Bellah (1966) invented the term "civil religion," and no one has yet coined a better phrase for it. Ironically, the analyst of civil religion turns into a prophet of civil religion at the end of his groundbreaking paper: Bellah endorses the very religion that he has historicized so carefully and invokes it to make his own moral point: Casting doubt on America's role in Vietnam, he reminds his fellow nationals that their, or rather, "our nation stands under higher judgment"; and he then proceeds to turn this American civil religion into a universal truth (pp. 17–18). A religion that convinces even the analyst must be powerful indeed.

Anderson and Bellah have taken us a long way from the naive belief that the state is but a secular business to service worldly needs. The nation-state tends to be secular-*ist*, but it is by no means secul-*ar*. That is, it pushes churches and worship into the private sphere, but the resulting vacuum of mystical rhetoric and ritual is quickly filled up with state-made quasi religion. The nation of each state is constructed as an imagined community, as if it were a supremely moral superethnos writ large, and the nation-state relies upon a web of symbolic values, places, and times that is nothing short of religious. What can this tell us about the multicultural project?

To get to the multicultural future, we must engage the state as more than a neutral stage on which things either do or don't happen. It is one of the cornerstone problems of the multicultural triangle, not its immovable center. This is so because the nation-state is neither ethnically neutral nor religiously neutral. The best exploration of this quasi-religious dimension of the state that has appeared since Bellah (1966) is Werner Schiffauer's (1993) comparison between America and Britain, Germany and France. Schiffauer implies, but he does not use, the notion of civil religion when he compares the four nation-states. Instead, he chooses the less emotive terms "civil culture" or "civil society" to discern the quasi-religious foundations of different national consciousnesses. His results, however, could fill a book on civil religions.

All civil religions, or civil societies, try to solve the same problem that faces all Western nation-states: how to square free competition with limiting boundaries. Western societies glorify the free and rational exchange of all that is useful. Ideas and favors of power are exchanged in the political forum, economic goods are exchanged in the market place, and traditions and rethinkings about all of these are exchanged on the cultural stage, be it that of theaters or newspapers, TV networks or video shops. This is the most radical system of free exchange known in human history, but it is also the most impudent. It forbids a politician to promote the power of his family, it outlaws a businessman who wants to line his friends' pockets, and it even suspects nepotism when media personalities favoritize their sons, daughters, or friends. Competition has to be public, anonymous, and absolute. This modern rule goes against every old intuition we have. Why should anyone strive for power, or for money or prestige, when they cannot pass it on to the people they know longest and love best? The logic is inhuman, and so it needs boundaries. It needs to have outsiders, where the rational charity stops; if it has none, it will create some. How these outsiders are created, however, is a matter for each civil society on its own. Americans and Brits, French and Germans, and all other nation-staters to boot, have each created their own civil culture and civil religion to draw a line somehow.

In the United States, where Bellah had done the groundwork, the case appeared most special to Schiffauer, too. U.S. civil society makes a cult of the freedom of each individual to do better than anyone else. Everyone is there to fight, and the state elites are to keep out of the scrum. Whether success is achieved by using ethnic networks or religious ones, family networks or parties, makes little difference: Everyone is there to succeed, and whoever succeeds may pass on his success to anyone he likes. The civil religion behind this is a faith, rather more Judeo-Protestant than Catholic, that humans are born, but Americans are reborn.

In Europe, there are more ancient barriers against this counter-intuitive competition of all against all, no matter who they are or whom they like. On the face of it, this should have meant less emancipation for minorities, but in reality, and perhaps paradoxically, it delivered vastly more in a shorter time. There is no such thing in Europe as an "urban underclass," an American code term for ethnic or religious minorities that are excluded in their entirety from the blessings of civil equality. Half of the paradox is explained by the long-standing socialist traditions within European nation-states. The model of the welfare state has been able to buy in most minorities in most countries. The other half of the paradox is resolved by examining the range of European civil cultures.

In Britain, the dominant civil culture does not expect one norm to rule absolute, even the base norm of individual success. Rather, its civil religion is based on a faith in differences, historically grown and never standardized. If America were like a rodeo, where each rider may choose his own helpers but is judged on his own, Britain would be a soccer tournament. Everyone should fight for a team and fight for it squarely but fairly. Teams, be they ethnic minorities or religious ones, should stick together at all costs, and any individualism is suspected of selfishness. The good citizen fights tough, plays fair, and thinks of his community as a whole. The civil ethos is adversarial; it views fair confrontation as the most honest way to decision making. These decisions evade matters of principle and instead tend to be pragmatic and particularist. Motorbikers must wear helmets, but Sikh motorbikers may wear their traditional turban; school students must wear uniforms, but Muslim schoolgirls may wear their headscarf, as long as it is in the uniform colors. The dominant idea of freedom is not an equality of all, but enough acceptable deals to satisfy each community in its own way. The fight for emancipation is not an individualist battle, as it is in America; it is community based, and even collective outbursts can be neutralized as a sign that, after all, the team is sticking together—"as it should."

If Germany were ever shaken by "race riots" on the British scale, it would probably die of shame as a nation. After their grandparents' generation with its Nazi state killed all the minorities in their midst, postwar Germans have remained frightened of political violence in general, and of ghetto building and community tensions in particular. The dominant civil culture owes as much to this horrible past as to the 1960s' influx of migrants, mainly from the Catholic Mediterranean and Muslim Turkey. It has reacted with a peculiarly moralist, or ethicized, ideal of freedom. It falls to each individual, whether national or foreigner, to cultivate a sense of responsibility for the common good, and indeed to seek his own good in what is best for all. Any collective particularism, as in the British case, or any self-promoting individualism, as in the American case, are frowned upon as irresponsible or selfish. These attitudes are criticized because they fall short of the dominant moralist ethos. Schiffauer's analysis strikes home to me in every point, yet I want to add two more points that confirm it. The first deals with shame, the second with competence. The stress that Germans place upon personal ethics is not so much an emphasis directed toward the inside as an emphasis broadcast toward the outside. Almost all Germans wish to be seen as postracist, postethnic, and postnationalist. The touchstone of their national self-respect is the recognition granted by outsiders, rather than by natives or migrants, that "the Germans are like everyone else." Most Germans feel that both their civic culture and their democratic credentials are still subject to the judgment of the world, that is, of nonnationals. Given the history of their nation-state, which required one hundred years of near-endless wars to put on the map, this culture of collective guilt is not surprising. What is surprising, however, and also reassuring, is the culture's dependence on the judgment of others. This dependence also explains one of the most striking characteristics of German civil culture. When all democratic means of resolving conflicts fail, the power of decision must be given, not to the people at large, but to committees of experts. When different sectional interests cannot be reconciled, then the popular will turns to independent professional experts or technocratic committees to provide a responsible compromise. While experts in Britain are expected to be on tap, their colleagues in Germany are always on top.

If German civic culture puts a prize on individual morals, its French counterpart seeks its strength in universal and anonymous competition regulated by an absolute equality of rules. The font of all liberty is equality and the shared faith in reason as such. While each minority in Britain may fight for its own particular deal, all minorities in France are expected to share this common faith in a centralist and antiparticularist cult of one metareligious rationality. The French revolutionaries turned the cathedral of Paris into a Temple of Reason, and the French state elites have kept reinventing this civil religion of One Reason for All. It is as if the French Republic, which replaced dynastic absolutism with the absolute value of citizenship, had declared ethnic and religious loyalties illegal for all times. Consider, for instance, the following confession of French national faith, written by the Minister of Education and published in France's most established newspaper, *Le Figaro* (Bayrou 1994). Its purpose was to reason the decision that schoolgirls of Muslim faith must be barred from wearing headscarves at school. Its text, which I have taken the liberty to *interpret in italics*, is civil religion at its most exclusive:

Ministerial Decree to All Directors of State Schools

In France,
the national project
and the republican project
have conjoined with each other
around a certain idea of citizenship.

Here, where Muslims are foreigners,
the politics of right-wingers
as well as left-wingers
have closed ranks around
one idea of the nation-state.

This French idea of
the nation and the Republic
will by its nature respect
all convictions,
in particular those of religion,
politics, and cultural traditions.

This idea of Frenchmen,
whether right-wing or left-wing
must be assumed without question
to respect all private beliefs,
even those of Muslims,
foreigners, and ethnics.

But it
excludes the explosion
of the nation into
separate communities,
indifferent to each other,
and considering only
their own rules and
laws, and engaged
in simple coexistence.

But the idea by itself
makes it an act of subversion
to recognize within our state
a plurality of minorities
that do not share our ideas
because they are egoistic
and ethnocentric. They
threaten lawlessness since
they wish to live here
without becoming French.

The nation is not only a
collection of citizens

France is more than
a country full of people

The Multicultural Riddle

pursuing individual rights.
It is a community of destiny.

This ideal
is pursued first and foremost
at schools. . . .

This laicist and national ideal
is the very substance of the school
of the Republic
and the foundation of its duty
toward civic education.

This is why it is impossible
at school to accept
the presence and
the proliferation
of signs which are so ostensive
that their signification
is precisely
to separate certain students
from the rules of the
communal life of the school.

These signs are in themselves
elements of proselytism,
the more so as they are
accompanied
by a questioning of certain
courses or disciplines,
as they jeopardize
the security of students,

or as they lead to
disturbances in the
common life of the institution. . . .

who are guaranteed civil rights.
France is a religion.

This kind of nationalism
is what the state pays for
when it funds public schools.

This ideology, shared between
left-wing and right-wing,
is the very reason why
there are state schools
and the reason why
the state schools your children.

Therefore you have no right
to enjoy public schooling
if your daughters wear veils
because these veils spread
such offensive messages
of cultural difference,
that we fear
you might opt out of
the one-nation agenda
of our state schools.

Things like veils are
tools of converting others,
especially because sometimes
girls with veils refuse
lessons in sports, swimming,
and music. Further,
the wearing of veils can
lead to violence by right-wing
French students,
who might get hurt,

or they can disturb
the purpose of a nationalist
state school.

The Nation-State, II: Business or Temple?

The presence of more discreet signs, expressing merely the attachment to a personal conviction cannot be subject to the same reserves. . . .

[I decree this] to explain . . . the double movement of respect for convictions and firmness in the defense of the republican project of our country.

To wear a little cross or crescent
round one's neck is
allowed, as long as it shows
religion as a strictly
private matter.

The state draws this line to show
one thing in particular:
Religion is fine
as long as you keep it private;
but even the left-wing demands
that the school must function
in the service of the nation.

The interpretation I have added has not been authorized by Maître Bayrou (1994), although I have cross-checked its sense and tact, so far as the original has any, with the help of some French students, all of them Christian. What matters about this brief analysis is to see how replete with quasi-religious meanings and faiths the nation-state can be. Its civil cultures and civil religions differ markedly from state to state, and the mutlicultural riddle is thus posed differently in each. The American rodeo, where each individual is out for himself; the British soccer field, where individuals are to play "fair but tough" for special team advantages; the German kindergarten with its high moral tone; the French dance around the secularist Golden Calf—each of these approaches, and even defines, minorities in a different way. The multicultural riddle is thus not only a riddle for the nation-state but also a riddle about the nation-state as such.

To get maximum benefit from this rethinking of the first corner of the multicultural triangle, let me summarize the process so far and also foreshadow what is to come. The multicultural triangle describes three problematic relationships: nation-state versus ethnicity, nation-state versus religion, and ethnicity versus religion. The former two we have scutinized; the latter remains to be investigated.

If nation-state and ethnicity make a problematic pair, this is due to the romantic heritage of the concept of nation. This heritage distinguishes ethnicities as if they were biological identities; it then equates these biological identities with whole cultures; and it finally postulates that the fulfillment of an ethnic identity is to become a state-making nation. In this way, the romantic mythology of the nation-state, as an ethnos turned nation turned state, keeps producing the seeds of its own destruction. The more that state elites play the national card, the more they encourage marginalized ethnics to play the secessionist card: "If you ethnic lot have your state, then our ethnic group wants its own state, too." Examples can be seen in a number of ethnic secessionist movements: In the United States, one may think of the Hawaiian or Puerto Rican independence movements, and in Europe, one may think of the effective partition of Belgium into three ethno-national substates; the gradual partition of Britain into Wales, Scotland, and England; the Kurdish nationalist struggle in Turkey and neighboring countries; and, most dramatically of course, the explosion of Yugoslavia into five ethnic states and Bosnia into three.

If nation-state and ethnicity are two conflicting ideologies because of the romantic heritage of the state, then nation-state and religion conflict because of the rationalist heritage of the state. The more the modernizing state had to justify its unprecedented concentration of power and wealth, the more it had to push religion out of the public sphere. This process is known as secularization, that is, the process of pushing religion out of public life and banishing it to the private sphere of each citizen—something that citizens do in their spare time and that has no political relevance. This is discussed in chapter 7, in which it is argued that the modern states did indeed turn secular-*ist*, but they became far from secul-*ar* themselves. They acted secularist in that they pushed churches and religious minorities out of the political space, but they were quick to fill the void with their own religious ideas about nationhood and personhood. The two are not as different as they sound: Each project of a nation-state must create a community of individuals, and it needs to shape these individuals and offer them a sense of being a moral self within that new community. This requires shared values that people must come to regard as their own. The more they do so, the more they will credit even their sense of moral self to the moral community of the nation. In the end, the moral self and the moral community of the nation-state become indistinguishable and are experienced as one and the same thing. It is then that people can stake their whole moral self-respect upon risking or ruining their lives for their fatherland and even volunteer to "die so that the nation may live" (Lincoln). At this point, the replacement of religion by nationalism is complete.

Yet even so, this replacement act was only ever partly successful. Religion remains one the problems that every nation-state has to face. It is not so easy to deal with people, whether they are citizens or not, who think that religion is the ultimate and absolute source of morality, more ultimate and more absolute than even the state. Why else would national constitutions absolve conscientious objectors from the duties of national defense, and why else would lawmakers tread so carefully in the moral matters of abortion, euthanasia, and even the propagation of condoms? To give to Caesar what is Caesar's and to God what is God's is a classic way of talking away the problem at hand: States make laws, and religions have Laws. This is one reason why religious moralities have always clashed, and will continue to clash, with civic moralities required and sanctioned by states. Religious conviction is the oldest problem of the modern nation-state, and religious difference the most intractable. We shall return to this strange battle in chapter 6.

Finally, to scrutinize the third interrelation between the corners of the multicultural triangle, we need to consider both ethnicity and religion as cultural identities. Both of these identities raise principles of entitlement and rights that stand against the nation-state logic of civil rights; this much is clear. Yet the matter gets more explosive still when ethnic distinctions and religious distinctions are made to coincide. In the United States, this happened early on: African Americans had their own religions to start with; they flocked to non-Episcopal churches when they gained the freedom to do so, and have since then strengthened ethnic demarcations with religious ones, both Christian and Muslim. Hispanic Americans, likewise, have resisted absorption into the ambit of the Anglo-Catholic or Irish-Catholic hierarchies and have reasserted their ethnic distinctiveness also on the religious terrain. The double marking of a dividing line, to render it both ethnic and religious at the same time, has been largely a matter of conscious action in the United States. On the whole, Americans could follow their own counsel in deciding whether one boundary line was enough, or whether two were better than one. In Europe, the reinforcement of ethnic boundaries by religious ones has usually been imposed upon minorities by the state. One may think of the most terrifying examples here. Jewish people in Germany were forced, by the Nazi regime, to view their religious difference as an "ethnic" or "racial" difference. They had no choice in this, and present-day Germans, no matter how much the world has changed, cannot treat Jews as if they were simply another religious minority among others. Bosnian Muslims, another example, had no choice about being styled into one among six Yugoslav nationalities, as opposed to a cross-national religious category. The choice was dictated to them when President Tito, probably the greatest champion of multiculturalism as the civil religion of a dictatorship, came up against the end of his state-making powers. Here again, there is no point in hoping that Bosnian Muslims will ever see themselves as Muslim Bosnians, that is, view religion as a category and nationality as a group. Similar problems can be discerned in

The Nation-State, II: Business or Temple?

Israel, too: Here again, it is the state elite that defines who is a Jew, who is an Israeli, who is a non-Jewish Israeli, and who is a non-Israeli Jew. As soon as the boundaries between religion and ethnicity are pushed together until they seem to coincide, all equality is a dream of the past. No multiculturalist can want this, and we therefore need to rethink our remaining two basics, ethnicity and religion. This is the task of the next two chapters.

Notes

1. The tune can be found under "Parry: op. 208" or "Elgar: arr. Parry" in almost all English-language hymnals around the world. It was first sung in public at a *Fight for Right* demonstration in London, in March 1916.

2. A more recent assessment of Bellah's findings about the civil religion of the United States has been worked out by Gehrig (1981).

Further Reading

Bellah, Robert. 1966. "Civil Religion in America." *Daedalus: Journal of the American Academy of Arts and Sciences* 95: 1–21.

Schiffauer, Werner. 1993. "Die *civil society* und der Fremde— Grenzmarkierungen in Vier Politischen Kulturen." Pp. 185–99 in *Schwierige Fremdheit. Ueber Integration und Ausgrenzung in Einwanderungslandern*, eds. F. Balke et al. Frankfurt/Main: Fischer. The author has kindly agreed to make an English translation available on the internet: "The Civil Society and the Outsider": http://viadrina.euv-frankfurt-o.de/~anthro/veronli_s.html.

5

Ethnicity: Blood or Wine?

Not Biological Essence, but Cultivated Ferment

When you're ashamed, you go red.
When you're cold, you go blue.
When you're sick, you go yellow.
When you're jealous, you go green.

And YOU? have the CHEEK?
to call me coloured??

(Anonymous poem circulating at a school
in Southall, London, ca. 1990)

IN COMING CLOSER to a multicultural understanding of ethnic identity, this anonymous poem may seem a very light-hearted starting point. But like so many creations of popular culture, it is worth a second look. For one, it questions an ethnic category, namely, "coloured," which is used by outsiders, usually "whites," to label some sort of otherness. The label is in common use, but people can reject ethnic labels imposed on them, and ethnicity is thus a matter of contestation. The way in which this contestation is argued is even more astute: The writer applies color terms to "white" people. Depending on their physical and mental states, people cease to be white and take on different colors; this shows that color identities, like all other identities, are a matter of situation and context. I may see and present myself, or be seen and received as, an exemplar of different colors at different times and in different contexts. By treating ethnicity as the same as color, the poem thus shows ethnicity as a matter of contestation within variable contexts, and thus as a social relationship.

This understanding may sound surprising at first. Most of us get one ethnic label at birth, and we retain it or reject it for the rest of our lives. Yet there are plenty of exceptions, if we may call them so for the moment. Many individuals of "mixed descent," that is, people combining locally unusual phenotypical appearances, are used to being shunted to and fro between different categories. Quite apart from such examples of "ambiguous ethnicity" on an individual plane (Benson 1981), different ethnic classifications and self-classifications can be in conflict with each other, even in one local area. I have described elsewhere (Baumann 1996) how the citizens of Southall, a multiethnic suburb of London, were locked in a passionate public debate on whether "Asians" were to be counted among the category of "Black" citizens.

The most systematic examples of the social plasticity of ethnic labels have tended to come from outside the Western nation-states, and this has historical reasons.[1] They are so impressive, however, that even a book on multiculturalism in the West has to take some account of them. A classic early example was Clyde Mitchell's (1956) analysis of *The Kalela Dance* as invented and performed by Bisa migrants on the African Copperbelt, now Zambia. This dance, which had not existed in the tribal home-lands and was consciously innovative and modernist, asserted a Bisa ethnic identity in the new and multiethnic mining com-pounds. Bisa ethnicity was thus not some tribalist hangover from a rural past, but a conscious and new reaction to multiethnic competition. An even more influential analysis of other exam-ples remains Fredrik Barth's (1969) collection *Ethnic Groups and*

Ethnicity: Blood or Wine?

Boundaries. The key point here was to wrench social science research away from its tribalist preoccupation with the "cultural stuff" that ethnic groups may share and to focus instead on the boundaries that separated ethnic groups. The "cultural stuff," in fact, very often showed as much overlap with neighboring groups as it showed variety within the boundaries. What made an ethnic identity "ethnic," therefore, was to be sought in the social processes of maintaining boundaries that the people themselves recognized as ethnic. With the focus shifted in this way, Barth and his collaborators found the most impressive evidence, not only of ethnic boundaries being maintained but also of individuals crossing these boundaries in systematic ways. In Pakistan, a Pathan can become recognized as a Baluch (Barth 1969); in Sudan, a Fur can assume the ethnic identity of a Baggara (Haaland 1969); in Southeast Asia, Chinese and various migrant groups can be incorporated into the Yao ethnic group (Kandre 1967). What studies such as these have shown time and again is that ethnicity is not what we thought it was. It is not, as Glazer and Moynihan (1975) still had it in their first reader, "the character or quality of an ethnic group" (p. 1), if that phrase is taken to mean the character or quality of its members; rather, "ethnicity is essentially an aspect of a relationship, not a property of a group," and it is "constituted through social contact," as Eriksen (1993, 12, 18) put it with perfect lucidity. In the end, we cannot even predict which differences will be considered ethnic by the people we study and which will be viewed as a matter of, say, social class. Yet this awareness has been extremely slow to spread beyond the confines of social science classes, and the commonsense view of ethnicity as a personal property acquired by birth has remained largely unchallenged in public debate. There are two reasons for this, and they need to be spelled out to move the multicultural debate beyond a restrictive view of ethnicity.

The examples that show ethnicity as a socially pliable construction will not, at first sight, convince the commonsense reader. They look like the odd exceptions that, as common sense has it, confirm the rule. To overcome this intuitive skepticism, let us give a brief thought to the place of "exceptions," using the commonsense example of a football match watched by a Martian. Most football matches are played for the possession and goaling of one ball, the same from beginning to end. A commonsense observer from Mars would therefore think that any one particular match is played for its one particular ball—much as if the ball were the trophy. It takes an exception, namely when a ball is replaced in midgame, to turn our commonsense Martian into a scientific Martian. Having taken due account of the one exception observed, the Martian will understand that what matters is not the individual ball, but any ball whatsoever that conforms to the abstract rules of the game. Since ethnicity has been shown to be situational, contextual, and contestable in all cases of doubt, then this must change our whole perception of the game. The problematic cases are no longer those where ethnicities are socially plastic, but those where they are not. This makes sense not only from a philosophical perspective, which advises us to study exceptions to understand the rules, but also from a political perspective. Ethnic boundaries have become less pliable in the West than they were among the Baluchis, the Baggara, or the Yao. We are indeed surrounded by an Apartheid logic of ethnicity, as if some god had created different colors, each with their own culture, on different days of the Creation Week. For a multiculturalist, this is a bad and philosophically untenable start. Yet we ourselves will all too often base our reasoning upon it.

This brings me to the second reason why we still battle on with this falsely restrictive idea of ethnicity. To find the roots of this fallacy, the Harvard political scientist Joseph Rothschild (1981) coined the term "ethnopolitics" to describe a process that took shape from the 1960s onward. He defined it as a process of "mobilizing ethnicity from a psychological or cultural or social datum into political leverage for the purpose of altering or *reinforcing* . . . systems of structured inequality between and among ethnic categories. [In this process, ethnopolitics] stresses, ideologizes, reifies, modifies, and sometimes virtually re-creates the putatively distinctive and unique cultural heritages of the ethnic groups that it mobilizes" (Rothschild 1981, 2–3; italics mine).

Ethnicity is thus transformed from a classificatory boundary, chosen or imposed as the case may be, into a substantive and unified group heritage, identified by its supposedly unified culture, again chosen or imposed as the case may be. This process is not entirely new; witness the hardening of tribal attitudes in times of warfare or competitive pressures. What is new about twentieth-century ethnopolitics, however, is that they politicize quasi-tribal differences within nation-states—precisely those nation-states that were expected to overcome ethnic divisions through equal citizenship. On the sociological plane, this might be the strangest development of the century. To appreciate how strange it is, consider the certainty of Max Weber ([1912] 1978), one of the founding fathers of the social sciences,[2] who wrote four generations ago: "All in all, the notion of 'ethnically' determined social action subsumes phenomena that a rigorous sociological analysis . . . would have to distinguish carefully. . . . It is certain that in this process [of examination] the collective term 'ethnic' would be abandoned, for it is unsuitable for a really rigorous analysis" (p. 395).

Was Weber singularly wrong in his otherwise proven sociological judgment, or has something gone badly wrong with the way in which we have come to view the idea of ethnicity? I suggest that the answer is yes in both cases, and we must ask how this could happen. There are at least two answers to this: one political, the other cognitive. The first answer is given, in its shortest if rather jargonized form, by Chicago anthropologists Jean and John Comaroff (1992): "[I]n systems where 'ascribed' cultural differences rationalize structures of inequality, ethnicity takes on a cogent existential reality. It is this *process of reification* . . . that gives it the [false] appearance of being an autonomous factor in the ordering of the social world" (p. 61; italics mine).

To crack this jargon, imagine a nation-state, whether South Africa or your own, where people believe that differences in thinking, behavior, or taste can be known in advance: "Because" you differ in looks, you must differ in mind. These differences, ascribed by others rather than achieved or created by the people so judged, can be used as false reasons to discriminate against them. As soon as this nonsense gets established, both the racists and the victims of ethnicism begin to believe that ethnicity is a real thing, inherent in persons and causing the inequalities among them. This, of course, is not only politically bad; it is also intellectually false. If racists use looks or roots to predict a person's behavior, they are clearly wrong on both counts. Yet antiracists, too, can use that false logic. By tracing discrimination to ethnic distinctions as if these distinctions were objectively real, antiracists reinforce the belief that ethnic differentiations are really absolute: As soon as discrimination is fought on an ethnic platform, "the very fact that such action is conducted by and for groups marked by their cultural identities confirms the [false] perception that these identities *do* provide the only available basis of collective . . . action" (Comaroff and Comaroff 1992, 62–63).

This process is why I emphasized the phrase *"or reinforcing"* in the quotation from Rothschild's *Ethnopolitics.* If racists play the false card of ethnic absolutism, then antiracists are tempted to play the same card in return. Yet playing this ethnic joker has the same pernicious effect on both players and watchers alike: Ethnicity is made to appear as if it were about absolute and natural differences, instead of relative and cultural choices of difference making or differentiation. Even the way in which the Comaroffs use the word "cultural" here will have to be questioned later on. Just as inequality and behavior are not caused by ethnic differentiations, so culture, too, is an independent variable in the multicultural triangle. We will elaborate upon this in chapter 7. In consulting the Comaroffs, we have seen one reason why ethnic discrimination is so hard to overcome: If one responds to it by ethnic mobilization, one plays the same card as the ethnicists themselves, and unless one is careful, one risks feeding the very monster one set out to kill. Yet beyond this political reason, there is a cognitive reason why the battle for interethnic equality cannot be fought on the basis of ethnicity alone. This consideration goes to the very heart of what multiculturalism is to achieve. Is multiculturalism the freedom *of cultures* or the freedom *to culture?* This last act of rethinking, too, will inform chapter 7.

The second reason why ethnopolitics could pass as the only way to democratic equality is cognitive in the widest sense, as opposed to political in the narrow sense. The Comaroffs have already hinted at it in noting *"this process of reification."* Both sides in the reformation of our society, racists as well as multiculturalists, have fallen victim to the cognitive error of the highest order there is: the error of reification. To know this term, which means thingification, or turning concepts into things, is probably the most important step in turning a person into a social scientist. The best explanation is this very old one: "Reification is the apprehension of human phenomena as if they were things, that is, . . . the apprehension of the products of human activity *as if* they were something other than human products—such as facts of nature. . . . Man, the producer of a world, is apprehended as its product, and human activity as an epiphenomenon of non-human processes" (Berger and Luckmann 1967, 106).

Ethnicity is the product of people's actions and identifications, not the product of nature working by itself. This is why ethnicity is not about blood as such or ancestry as such. Rather, it is about the cultivation and refinement of all the possibilities first given by nature, but not finished by nature. In seeking a contrast to the "blood" view of ethnicity, I have chosen to liken it to wine for several reasons. Wine is made of grapes, and it enjoys the reputation of a natural product, just as ethnic identities are usually associated with natural bonds as between forebears and descendents. Yet nature itself does not produce wine, just as little as ancestry by itself produces ethnicity: The natural ingredients need to be added to in order to achieve a process of fermentation, just as ethnic categorizations need political and economic interests to turn them into markers of identity that can operate in daily life. At the next stage, wine needs the right conditions to mature, just as ethnicity needs particular social conditions to acquire meaning among those who see themselves as sharing it. Finally, a wine will develop different flavors at different temperatures, and at some it will cease to be wine and turn to vinegar or water. Ethnicity, likewise, takes on different connotations and meanings, depending on the social climate in which it is experienced. Ethnic identities can be stressed or unstressed, enjoyed or resented, imposed or even denied, all depending on situation and context. Both wine and ethnicity are thus creations of human minds, skills, and plans—based on some natural ingredients, it is true, but far beyond anything that nature could ever do by itself.

This does not mean, of course, that either wine or ethnicity are in some way unreal. Most of us have very little choice but to relate to the ethnic identities that others tell us we have, and the anthropologist Peter Worsley (1984) was right when he criticized "many interactionist studies of ethnicity . . . [because] choice is assumed to be the crucial social fact. Life, it would seem, is a market or a cafeteria" (p. 246). The point is well taken. I can be discriminated against because of other people's ethnic criteria whether I endorse them or not, just as I will get sick if someone forces a bottle of wine down my throat. The point, however, is clear: What makes me sick is not natural grape juice, but the fermented product of human social activity.

"Pure blood," however, is precisely the label under which ethnicity is sold by ethnopolitical movements. It is instructive here to glance at two outstanding studies of such movements to see how they function. One is a study of the Breton ethnic movement in France written by social anthropologist Maryon McDonald (1989); the other, written by cultural anthropologist Richard Handler (1988), deals with the ethno-nationalist movement of the Québecois in Canada.

The Breton ethnic movement argues that the inhabitants of the Brittany peninsula of northwestern France are not French but form part of a "Celtic nation" that once stretched across Europe in a great swathe from Ireland to present-day Turkey (McDonald 1989). In northwestern Europe, it is argued, there remain the "Celtic nations" of the Irish in Ireland; the Scots, Welsh, Manx, and Cornish in Great Britain; and, last but not least, the Bretons in France. What we are dealing with is, of course, a classification of languages, rather than people or even their ancestors. Yet "the definition of certain languages as 'Celtic' is widely taken to imply a distinct category of people, the Celts, who share a common origin in . . . flesh and blood" (p. 97). Since the vast majority of Celtic-speakers use English or French far more often than their Celtic languages, the restitution and public recognition of these languages form the principal demand and ambition of ethnopolitical activists. Two things are remarkable in this endeavor: The activists appeal to a pseudobiological foundation of Breton identity, and they strive at a language that is "purified" from the "contaminating" influences of French, English, or even bilingualism (pp. 152–74). It is a purity long lost by the rural people to whom the activists promise cultural liberation, and this imbalance between the rural people and the urban-based militant ethno-nationalists goes very much further, as McDonald concludes in her charitable final evaluation:

> The movement has helped to create a new space of glamour that the ordinary Breton-speaker can occupy, and that in itself is laudable. It remains the case, however, that it is the mili-

65

tants who have appropriated the virtues of the Breton-speaking minority, and who dress themselves in its history, and who reap much of the benefit of the modern minority cause. It is they who are at the centre of things, it is they who do the defining. (pp. 315–16)

There are thus two mechanisms at work in such an ethnopolitical transformation of linguistic inheritance into ethnic identity: It invokes biology to argue culture, and it is run by activists who are socially far removed from the people whose lives they seek to purify and style into "ethnic identities." A third mechanism that works under the surface is that all ethnopolitics has implications for the gendering of personalities. In a section wonderfully entitled "Femininity: From Cow-Shit to Finery" (pp. 245–49), McDonald shows ethnopolitics as a "pervasive system of thought in which an essential and inherent 'masculinity' and 'femininity' have been forged . . . from dichotomies which also commonly construct majority/minority relations" (p. 310).[3]

The restoration, or rather, the new assertion of a newly defined purity, as well as the accompanying fear of some cultural contamination, are evident also in the ethnopolitics of the Québecois. Richard Handler (1988) found that "one can speak without exaggeration of a pervasive fear of pollution and contamination—metaphors frequently used by the nationalists themselves" (p. 47). The trouble is, they are not only used as metaphors but also are used as tools for imposing cultural conformity on those with less power. The ethnopolitical leaders knew full well "that a disturbing number of Quebec's francophone youth were powerfully drawn to the English-language culture of the United States, and that a significant minority did not consider their language to be a valued cultural possession" (p. 184). Yet such dissidents show all the more clearly, in the logic of ethno-national conformity, that francophone schooling must be made compulsory for all.

Ethnicity: Blood or Wine?

The same compulsion also applies to those 20 percent of the population who have migrated to Quebec from countries where French is not spoken. Admittedly, one cannot turn them into "ethnic" Québecois, for only so-called "blood" can do that; what one can do, however, is turn them into Québecois minorities, rather than Canadian ones. Thus, the ministry responsible for immigration sees in its minorities "so many ways of being Québecois" (p. 178), and in its multicultural pamphlets, "each group is also given a history in relation to Quebec, a rhetorical ploy which constructs the group as a *Québecois* minority, . . . integrated into yet clearly bounded within Quebec society" (p. 180). The ethnopolitical fear of cultural dissent affects all minorities, even those whom one counts as outsiders.

Whether we take evidence from the colonized world or from Western nation-states, it points to the same conclusion. Ethnicity and ethnopolitics rely on rhetorics that trace cultural differences to biological differences; they aim at purifying and canonizing the cultural essences that they have reified, and those who promote them show little regard for dissent in promoting their policies of cultural unity. This does not, of course, make them any worse than nation-state nationalists: The Breton activists are doing much the same as the French state elites, and the Québecois much the same as the nationalist anglophone elites. They only do it for different kinds of ideals, that is, for an ethnopolitical opposed to a nation-state unity. What the data make clear, however, is that ethnopolitical unity is no more natural, biological, or indeed tolerant of dissent, than is national unity.

Having de-essentialized our understanding of ethnicity, it remains to perform a similar operation of rethinking the third corner of the multicultural triangle. Just as ethnicity is easily essentialized as if it were a matter of blood, rather than a pliable social creation, so religion, too, is widely essentialized as if it were about immutable sacred texts, rather than the convictions of living and changeable people.

Notes

1. Studies of ethnicity began in the colonized world long before they
   became common in the West. Partly, this is because cultural anthropologists focused their work on the colonized countries until the
   1960s. Partly, ethnicity was higher on the political agenda wherever
   the nation-state was a new foundation and urbanization and industrialization were recent phenomena.

2. Like all sciences, social sciences, too, are credited, by the usual patriarchal histories, with having two or three fathers and no mothers at all.
   It is nice to know, however, that single-sex relationships can be
   thought to be so fertile even by patriarchal minds.

3. An evocative example of such new processes of gendering can be found
   at festive evening gatherings when "the women sit together at one end
   of a long table with their sweet cakes and sweet drinks and speak predominantly French, and the men pack together at the other end in a
   haze of cigarette smoke, eating cheap *pâté*, drinking hard liquor, playing dominoes or cards, and speaking predominantly Breton. While
   Anna at one end speaks French to the women, her husband at the
   other end speaks Breton to the men" (McDonald 1989, 248).

Further Reading

Handler, Richard. 1984. "On Sociocultural Discontinuity: Nationalism and
Cultural Objectification in Quebec." *Current Anthropology* 25 (1): 55–71.

McDonald, Maryon. 1986. "Celtic Ethnic Kinship and the Problem of Being
English." *Current Anthropology* 27 (4): 333–47.

6

Religion: Baggage or Sextant?

Not Immutable Heritage, but Positioning in Context

> There are as many Islams as there are situations that sustain it. (Aziz Al-Azmeh 1993, 1)
>
> [I]n the United States . . . there are at least seventeen distinct communities of Islamic expression. (Aminah McCloud 1995, 52)
>
> The basic . . . fallacy of *both* sociological *and* [non-academic] communalist versions is that they portray Muslim and Hindu values as reified systems. (Peter van der Veer 1994, 29)

LIKE ETHNICITY, religion, too, is often reified and essentialized as if it were the one thing beyond change. Such reifications often serve the interests of religious elites who wish to stem unwelcome social changes, or they may comfort believers who regard their religion as the only thing that has remained the same amidst all the turmoils of urban living, migration, and the multicultural challenge. Nonetheless, while all religions claim to have an immutable core, even the meaning of that core changes as it is reasserted in new circumstances. To repeat the same statement in new circumstances is to make a new statement.[1] This is why Aziz Al-Azmeh's contention, quoted here, is the only safe starting point. At first sight, this contention must sound shocking, and it may even sound blasphemous to some. Yet we would have no hesitation in applying this statement to the whole range of convictions that people use to guide their moral commitments: There are, quite clearly, as many socialisms, feminisms, commitments to environmentalism, and ideas about human rights as there are contexts that sustain them. Why, then, does it sound so strange to apply the same awareness of different contexts to Islam? Al-Azmeh has two answers to this.

On the one hand, it is the mainstream media and the mainstream politicians that, each in their own countries, talk about "*the* Muslim problem," and they find it useful to paint this problem as a global one. To say that "we British" or "we French" have a problem with the Muslims living among us would open a very unwelcome question: What is wrong with the British or the French? To say that "Islam" is a problem throughout the Western world allows them to put the blame on "Islam" as such and on Muslims wherever they are. On the other hand, and at the same time, it is also the advocates and the self-appointed representatives of Muslims who claim to speak for "*the* Muslim community" or indeed for Islam as such. It allows them to revel in their own importance, and it absolves them from the critical question of who, in fact, has asked them to be their public representatives.

This is a fateful convergence between Muslim-bashers and Muslim spokespersons. It has a number of unfortunate consequences, of which two are especially repressive: First, whatever a spokesperson may say about the views or attitudes of the Muslims he claims to represent is stylized into "*the* attitude of *the* Muslim community," as if all Muslims thought and behaved in the same way. Second, all those who disagree with their public representatives are ruled out of court as being "unrepresentative" Muslims, either bad because they are "sectarian" or bad because they are "secularized." What connects the pronouncements of Muslim-bashers such as the right-wing nationalists and the Muslim advocates is, in Al-Azmeh's words, a "culturalist view of religion" combined with a "tribalist view of culture" (1993, 8–9). The result is an "imaginary Islam" (1993, 1) that oppresses Muslims who have nothing to do with it.

To see the tangible dangers, one need only cast an eye over the so-called "religious conflicts" that Muslims have had to contend with outside the West. The dangers are most tangible on the Indian subcontinent, where two different nationalisms, one Indian and one Pakistani, pitched Muslims and Hindus against each other at the cost of several million lives. It may be comforting to know that most of these millions were killed more than a generation ago, when the colony of British India underwent partition into an officially secular India and an officially Muslim Pakistan. It is less comforting to know that this Hindu–Muslim conflict has continued to produce communalist violence and bloody persecutions ever since. Distilling the sociological lessons from this development of two "religious nationalisms," the Amsterdam anthropologist Peter van der Veer (1994) found an odd convergence. Both the communalists who started the violence and the academics who were supposed to explain it made the same mistake: No matter which side they came from, they caricatured "Muslim and Hindu values as reified systems" (p. 29). This kind of essentialist caricature can only serve one purpose in the end, that of essentializing the conflict itself. There are lessons to be learned from this when we speak of religion in the multicultural West of the future.[2]

Of the conflicts that Muslims have had to face in the West, the most dramatic to date was the so-called "Rushdie Affair," which started in 1989. To summarize the events briefly, the novel *The Satanic Verses*, written by avant-garde author Salman Rushdie, was declared by Muslim spokespersons in Britain to be blasphemous. They mobilized Muslims in the English city of Bradford to join organized protests, and protesters publicly burned a copy of the book. When another Muslim spokesman, this time the aging leader of the Iranian revolution, Ayatollah Khomeini, pronounced a religious edict (*fatwa*) of death upon the author, the European media constructed a confrontation that pitched Islam and all Muslims against Western civilization and all who believed in the freedom of speech. It was as if each Muslim, whether or not he had any interest in the book or in the Ayatollah Khomeini's interpretations of Islam, was to be put in the dock: "Are you for Islam and thus against freedom of speech, or are you for freedom of speech and thus a bad Muslim?" In this McCarthyite frenzy of locking people into false alternatives, the best British journalist wrote:

> [T]he only thing on which anti-Islamic liberals and their fun-
> damentalist opposite numbers agreed was that there was such
> a thing as a "Muslim community". "It" was either a threat to
> liberal civilisation as we know it, or "it" was a resurgent faith
> on the march. At the height of the affair, Muslims in Britain
> could be forgiven for wishing no one had ever thought them a
> community at all. (Ignatieff 1992, 17)

That they had been thought to be "one" community was precisely because of the mechanisms Al-Azmeh (1993) identified. What, we must therefore ask, can be done against such oppressive mechanisms? There are three answers that demand consideration. The first one must lie in a critical analysis of the false alternatives that media, politicians, and spokesmen combine to impose on the public. In this way, Peter van der Veer (1994, 179–91) has shown how spurious it is to force Muslims into a "holy battle" between one kind of holiness, that of the Qur'an, and another kind of holiness, that of the sacrosanct freedom of the Western high-brow novel. It is the choice that is wrong, not one or the other opinion among Muslims. The second answer must lie in a clear-headed empirical inquiry of how such climactic events as a book-burning comes to pass, and which powerful conflicts of interest lie behind them. In this way, British sociologist Yunas Samad (1992) has shown how the Bradford demonstrations were the result of two long-standing rivalries: one between Muslim religious leaders and Muslim political activists in Bradford, and the other between organizations from Iran and organizations from Saudi Arabia, which had both competed to finance Muslim opinion leaders in Britain for a very long time.

Third, we must get away empirically from the "imaginary Islam" Al-Azmeh (1993) traced to the combination of a "culturalist view of religion" and a "tribalist view of culture" (pp. 1, 8–9). The most lucid European example of such an empirical study comes from Werner Schiffauer, the German anthropologist who best combines research on Islam in Turkey with research on Turkish Muslims in a Western country. In a short but comprehensive article, Schiffauer (1988) demonstrates four particular changes in religiousness that could be observed between the Muslims of the Turkish village of Subay and their kin and friends that had migrated to Germany. On the plane of ritual, villagers' experience stressed the ancient communal character of all households participating in the same ceremonies in the life and seasonal cycles. In German cities, the rituals became conscious affirmations of a religious order, as opposed to the secular order in which migrants now found themselves. On the plane of political ideas, villagers professed some sympathy with applying Islamic Law (sheriat), but they felt none of the great hopes that migrants could attach to an Islamic reform of the law. On the plane of religious choices, villagers collectively agreed on a set canon of rules to be followed by all, while their migrant kin embarked on a far more individual search for truth, hotly debating their allegiances to different Muslim movements. On the plane of self-awareness, finally, villagers saw religious obligations as a debt to God that could be made up at any stage before one's death, especially as one grew more pious with age. To the migrants, religious merit appeared as a lifelong commitment to educating one's piety and a constant striving for religious growth.

Schiffauer's distinction of the four planes of change can be applied to many other cases, and the search for the causes of this change can broaden our perspective even further. He traces the changes to two factors: the community-based nature of Islam, and the migration of Muslims into a secular foreign society. Yet one does not need to single out Islam as a peculiarly communal religion by nature. What natures it might have in Subay may well be shared by all other faiths practiced in homogeneous village communities. Nor does one need to stress Subay people's migration into a Western diaspora; the same processes may well follow from the process of urbanization in their own country. Here, too, one often finds a new and peculiarly modernist tension that tints all religious conceptions, the distinction between a secularist nation-state reality and a religious utopia.

A skeptic might think, at this stage, that such arguments for the contextual plasticity of religion are overacademic, that they focus on subtle changes of emphasis and lose sight of the fundamental bedrock of faith that all believers share. Yet here, too, social reality is far more inventive than any sociological theory, and Islam is an ideal example. Consider, for a few minutes, the transformations in African American Islam. We do not know, and no one can possibly know, how many African Muslims there are in the United States. Aminah McCloud (1995), who wrote the most comprehensive survey, puts the figure at some "1.5 to 4.5 million persons" (p. 1), an astonishing margin of error. This uncertainty, however, has very good reasons, for no one can know who counts whom as a Muslim. Even the Nation of Islam, which most outsiders think is one movement, has fissioned into three movements that fight tooth and nail to discredit each other's claims. Even counting these three as one, McCloud has found:

> [T]here are at least seventeen distinct communities of Islamic
> expression. These communities can be differentiated in terms of
> (1) Islamic understanding—how they adhere to what has come

to be known in the Sunni Muslim world as the five pillars; . . . (2) whether the group has nation-building as its focus
rather than the wider Muslim community (here and abroad); and
(3) how they acknowledge the leader of the community. (p. 52)

Such an acknowledgment of a sectional leader can go so far as
to recognize him "as divinely inspired (i.e., as *mahdi* or messi-
ah)" (p. 52), and it can even entail "the notion that Fard
Muhammad, the [1920s] founder of [a particular] movement, was
God in person" (p. 73). Some of the sectional movements
exclude immigrants from Muslim countries outside the
American Nation of Islam; others welcome them (p. 71). Some
base their teachings on the Qur'an alone; others revere the Bible,
too (p. 81). Some keep Ramadan as the Muslim month of fasting;
others have replaced it with a "December Fast" (p. 81). Most
Muslims would be surprised to hear that these movements
entertain any "desire to avoid . . . heresy" (p. 5). Faced with such
a range of doctrinal variance, not to speak of the political and
"race"-related arguments that go with them, the social scientist's insistence on the socially pliable nature of all religion must
sound like a minimalist's version of plain common sense.[3]

Have we gone too far in letting burgeoning social realities correct our limited sociological imagination of religion as a thing
fixed once and for all? There will be readers, no doubt, who simply want to write off African American Islam as "one of those
strange things that happen abroad. The facts may threaten all
kinds of certainties, but in the end, let us discount them as mar-
ginal phenomena." Yet such a cavalier attitude is untenable for
two reasons at least. First, these exceptional phenomena have
exceptional social consequences. One need only recall the
Million Man March on Washington called by Louis Farrakhan
for the Nation of Islam. It drew together the largest number of
African American men ever seen in one place.[4] The second reason why community formations of Muslims in the United States

cannot be written off leads to a more fruitful revision of multi-cultural theory. It is obvious that African American Islam has been developed as a response to some very peculiar nation-state conditions: After two hundred years of black slavery, one hundred years of unsuccessful black emancipation, and the failure of several civil rights projects, the activists of the Black Power Movement turned to Islam as a redeeming moral and political force in the 1970s. The sociological lesson thus points to the interaction of the religious domain with the politics of the state. This perspective is theoretically telling.

If one needed any additional reason why religions must change as they are lived, one would find it in the existence of the nation-state itself. Not only can old nation-state elites misread the writing on the wall; progressive elites, too, can turn the nation-state into an obstacle of its own citizens' equality. With this observation, we return to the paradox of the nation-state that claims to be secular but is only secular-*ist* about the nonstate religions. We have touched on this problem in chapter 4, and a good case in point is the place of the "new" religions in Britain.

In Britain, as in other Western countries, Muslims, Hindus, and Sikhs have only established themselves in sizeable numbers over the past forty years. Just about half of them were born in the colonized world, and although the other half are younger people born in the West, they still face considerable problems of racism and discrimination. As we have seen in chapter 4, the civil religion and political culture of Britain encourages so-called minorities to strive for emancipation as if they were sports teams: They are approached as so-called "communities," and politicians, the media, and almost everybody else thinks of them as tightly knit "cultural groups" held together by the same traditions, value system, and history. It is perfectly clear that this is not true;[5] but this is the misperception under which they must hope to achieve civil emancipation, as well as the misperception under which British state elites try to "help" them. If you approach people by way of reifying their culture, the only certain thing you will achieve is a further reification of their culture. The same is true for reifying their religion, and there are three exceedingly simple steps to do this by political means. Although these steps have been documented most clearly in Britain, they can be recognized almost anywhere in the West.

The first step is to register congregations, that is, to declare a local temple or mosque, or else a particular faith as such, as the representative of a "community of culture." This means including some applicants and excluding others, much as the colonial censuses included some local distinctions, ruled out others, and imposed new ones on top of this selection (Appadurai 1993). Once this political movement has been set on its way, it must follow the dynamics of religious fissions and split ups. As bigger congregations split up into smaller ones, state practice will recognize some of these as additional "communities of culture" and will give them additional resources. If the first step is "divide and rule," the second is "serve to divide." Although the word is cumbersome, one could call this second process congregationalization, that is, the state actively helping to form new and more tightly bounded religious congregations by the promise of sectional emancipation. This promise does not come free, of course: The state, and especially the local state, expects these congregations to help pacify and placate the people thus singled out as special cases of "religious" discrimination as opposed to plain civic inequality. This is the third step, which may be called functional devolution. It means that the state devolves some of its own functions and duties to others, in this case, that it uses religious congregations to help it discharge its own public duties. It commonly does so by the agency of the local state, which channels earmarked funds to religious congregations that are then to spend the monies on their own youth work, libraries, community centers, and social services. The most extreme example was observed in London when a local authority asked temples and mosques to take care of the most fundamental duty of the state—to turn resident people into national citizens (Baumann 1996).

The British example may seem extreme, but other European states also have their own ways of seeking active cooperation with, and influence over, the congregations of the "new" religions. In Belgium, there is a central state register of recognized religions; for these, it is the state that pays the clergy's salaries. In the Netherlands, there are initiatives involving state universities in the training of Muslim clerics—much as was the case in the Dutch colonies with Muslim populations. These practices cast a strange light upon the nation-state's claim to being a secular enterprise. What is more important in this context, however, is what such state initiatives do to the religions concerned. It stands to reason that processes of registration, congregationalization, and functional devolution must change the conceptions that believers hold of their own, as well as of other, religions. The symbolic and practical significance of a mosque or a temple is transformed fundamentally when it assumes the role of channeling state resources and services.

As all the evidence shows, religion is thus not some cultural baggage that is taken along on migration wrapped, tied, and tagged; even when it is, it cannot be unpacked unchanged at the other end. Rather, one might compare religion to a compass: It provides a point of orientation, and it always points to the same objective pole. But the matter is even more complicated than that alternative metaphor might suggest. A compass points north, wherever you are. Yet the bearings of religious conviction and action will change as the users themselves change positions, or see them changed in their new contexts. It is more appropriate, therefore, to comprehend religion as a sextant, the instrument that sailors use to calculate their own position relative to a changing night sky. The sextant was reliable enough to lead Columbus to where India should have been, according to the maps of his day, but what the sextant indicates will always take account of the relative time and location of the navigators themselves. This relational aspect, which we already noted in our discussion of ethnicity, is thus equally clear in the case of religion.

Notes

1. The handiest example in the religious sphere comes from Remy Leveau (1988), a scholar who has documented the Muslim presence in France over the past thirty years. When the circumstances change, even such an "objective" fact as the existence of a mosque will take on a new meaning. When it was built between the two world wars, the grand central mosque of Paris represented the cosmopolitan splendor of a French empire ruling over a quarter of the Muslim world. When large Muslim communities came to settle in France beginning in the 1960s, the mosque came to signify something quite different: the presence, amidst the French, of a religious minority now considered alien, vast, and threatening (Leveau 1988).

2. The phenomenon of "religious nationalism" (van der Veer 1994) is most common in the formerly colonized countries, where resistance to colonial rule could only be articulated in religious terms, but decolonization produced nation-states in the image of the colonial powers. Examples can be seen in India and Pakistan, Afghanistan and the southern republics of the former Soviet Union, and the religio-national secession movements in East Timor, the southern Philipines, and Muslim northern China. The first entry of religious nationalism onto the Western scene happened with the disintegration of the former Yugoslavia, which produced a Catholic religious nationalism in Croatia, an Orthodox one in Serbia, and the destruction, between these two, of once-multicultural Bosnia.

3. The political and "race"-related variations are discussed by Magida (1996), Gardell (1996), and Kepel (1996). These variations can assume the starkest mythical contours, as with this legend of the creation of the "white race": It was Yacub, the Mighty Black Scientist born in 8400 BC and remarkably close to the later Mecca, who created whites to be his devils on earth. Such doctrines are interesting in two regards. For one, they show the techniques of conflating an ethnic boundary

with a religious one, as discussed at the end of chapter 4. Secondly, they can serve as an astonishing illustration of the philosophical point stressed by Charles Taylor (1994), namely, that all identities are formulated dialogically in exchange with a real or imaginary other (see chapter 9).

4. The success of the Million Man March on Washington, which took place in October 1995, has three reasons at least. In its name, it recalled the first March on Washington, organized by Martin Luther King for the Civil Rights Movement; it thus drew vastly more supporters than there are African American Muslims who follow Louis Farrakhan's Chicago branch of the Nation of Islam. Second, by its insistence that only men could take part, it could inflate the number of "silent supporters" who had been told to stay at home by the masculine leader to an uncheckable extent. Third, there was the content of Farrakhan's message, namely, that African American men needed to reform themselves morally to "deserve" equal rights as citizens. It is an open question how this last reason can be reconciled with the principle of equal rights, be they phrased as civil, community, or even human rights: I have never yet met anyone who wants to make any of these dependent upon an individual's moral merit. Who is to judge?

5. The internal diversity of these so-called "cultural groups" has been unfolded in a wide range of empirical studies, starting with Ken Pryce (1979), who first showed subdivisions in Britain's "Caribbean community," and Parminder Bhachu (1985), who showed them in Britain's "Asian community." That different cultural cleavages will cut across each other has been demonstrated first and compellingly by Sandra Wallman (1979) in the context of work relations and substantiated further by Pnina Werbner (1990) in the context of residential relations.

Further Reading

Schiffauer, Werner. 1988. "Migration and Religiousness." Pp. 146–58 in *The New Islamic Presence in Western Europe*, eds. T. Gerholm and Y. Lithman. London: Mansell.

7

Culture: Having, Making, or Both?

From an Essentialist through a Processual to a Discursive Understanding

The Age of Comparison. The less that people are tied by custom, the greater grows the inner movement of their motivations, the greater, accordingly, the outward unrest, the intermingling of people, the polyphony of intentions. Who, nowadays, is still subject to any strict compulsion to tie himself or his offspring to one particular place? Who, indeed, is subject to any strict compulsions at all? Just as all the styles of art are used side by side, so with all levels and kinds of moralities, customs, and cultures.—Such an era receives its importance from the fact that all different world-views, customs, cultures can be compared and lived out side by side.... This is the age of comparison! ... Let us understand the task of our age in as positive a way as we can: then future generations will thank us—future generations who will have gone both beyond the mutually separate original folk cultures and beyond the culture of comparison. (Friedrich Nietzsche [1878] 1968, 45; transl. mine)

IT IS HARD TO BELIEVE that the German philosopher Nietzsche should have written this analysis almost one hundred years before the word multiculturalism was even thought of. For whatever was wrong with Nietzsche, he envisioned living people as the active negotiators of culture and cultural difference. Such a view was unheard of when other prominent social thinkers were working out the "scientific" doctrines of colonial domination and underpinning them with racialist theories of "high cultures" and "low cultures." What Nietzsche was reacting to was, most probably, the urbanization of the West, in which the burgeoning cities attracted scores of new groups, each with their own "folk cultures." Far from entertaining some naive melting pot vision, Nietzsche predicted a period of cross-cultural comparison that, if all went well, would then give way to a new understanding of culture. All did not go well in Western history, and even a lot of present-day multicultural thinking has not gone beyond Nietzsche's stage of comparison, as we will see in chapters 8 and 9. The new understanding of culture that the long-dead philosopher predicted still has a long way to go; but one hundred years later, it is high time to sketch some of its requirements.

Nietzsche's reference point of rural European "folk cultures" thrown together in the ever-expanding "new" cities of London, Berlin, and New York provides a perfect starting point: Who, nowadays, would maintain that these "folk cultures" could either go on unchanged or would mingle in some magic melting pot? No matter which "folk" region any Western city dwellers trace their rural ancestries to, they will all agree, nowadays, that they share in the culture of Londoners, Berliners, and New Yorkers—that is, post-"folk" metropolitans. People may look for their "folk roots," of course; but the people who do so are undeniably metropolitans: Even in their search for "roots," they follow metropolitan-cultural routines and methods, expectations and theories. Witness the Anglos from America, Australia, and New Zealand who search for their ancestors in the computerized navy lists of the British Public Record Office; observe the diasporic Hibernians who fly to Ireland to see their ancestral cottages, painted white for the occasion by the Irish Tourist Board; or study the catalogs for the commercial tours put on for anyone who searches for their "cultural roots" in West Africa. Even the planned and conscious search for "cultural roots" is an entirely urban phenomenon, not to speak of the definition of culture that is rekindled in this ultramodern idea of "roots." We have seen as much in McDonald's (1989) analysis of the folky ethnic nostalgics among Breton intellectuals. Those who feel they have roots do not need to search for them, and many of those who "have" them want to get away from them. It is the uprooted who start and keep talking of roots. The transformation of "folk culture" from a rural given to an urban longing is a phenomenon of metropolitan culture, much as Mitchell observed in the Southern Africa *Kalela Dance* in 1956. I state the point strongly because it can serve as a model for the pending rethinking of culture in a multicultural setting.

Today's multiculturalism is no longer concerned with the "folk cultures" of white peasants flocking to cities run by other white people who despised them and often wanted them out again. The present-day challenge, both political and theoretical, is about three other concerns. The points of the multicultural triangle are about nationality as culture, ethnicity as culture, and religion as culture. All of these crumble as soon as one scratches the surface: Nationality as culture is neither postethnic nor postreligious; ethnicity as culture is based on culturally fermented commitments, not on raw genes; and religion as culture is not a matter of sacred rule books but of contextual bearings. Yet all three versions of culture share the same choice: whether culture is comprehended as a thing one has, or as a process one shapes. Until now, the more influential of the two theories is the essentialist one, which regards national cultures, ethnic cultures, and religious cultures as finished objects. Their features, it is thought, have been worked out through long historical processes, and they are thought now to influence and even shape the actions and thoughts of all their so-called members. In this view, culture, whether national, ethnic, or religious, is something one has and is a member of, rather than something one makes and reshapes through constant renewing activity. This essentialist view has two advantages in daily life. In dealing with children and other dissenters, it helps keep them on the straight-and-narrow: "Do as your culture says," it warns, "or you are a bad member or no member at all." In dealing with strangers, it helps one stereotype them with the greatest of ease and to make commonsense predictions of how these others might think and what they might do next. An American will act like an American, an ethnic like an ethnic, a Muslim like a Muslim. One need not ask who they are if one knows what they are. There is only one problem: How do I predict the opinions of anyone with a crosscutting or multidimensional identity? Will an African American Muslim behave and think like an American, like a black American, or like a Muslim? How will ethnic Albanian Muslims behave in Bosnia as opposed to Serbia? And what of the atheist Turkish-born Netherlander who, like so many other minorities, attends a Roman Catholic school?

This essentialist view of culture can be of no use for any kind of multicultural future or even analysis: It turns children into cultural photocopies and adults into cultural dupes. The fault is the same in both cases: It disregards the fact that we all practice more than one culture. We all participate in the keeping up, not to mention the remaking, of a national culture, an ethnic culture, and a religious one, and we probably participate in the culture associated with a region or a city, a particular language community, and a social category such as students or workers, feminists or motorbikers, surfers or punks—the list is endless. In the urbanized societies of the West, and in fact everywhere else in our urbanized world, different cultural cleavages do not run parallel to each other. Rather, they cut across one another to form an ever-changing pattern of what may be called "cross-cutting cleavages" (Baumann 1996). By criteria 1, one belongs to categories A and L; by criteria 2, to categories B and K; by criteria 3, one is, for that moment, only a C. Yet these criteria cut across each other, and consequently, the categories they define and the groups that people may form will cut across each other, too. People with odd crossover points are known as eccentrics: They defy people's normal expectations of which criteria go with what other criteria. Yet entertaining as eccentrics may be, the rest of us are twice as pluricentric when you consider some perfectly normal and everyday routines. Let us take one minute to trace a morning's worth of the multiple identities of Mr. Essentialist. In his office at nine, Mr. Essentialist says "Hi" to a lower-class colleague born in the same up-country region. Rather than stressing their distinction by class, he shares a joke about their city-slicker colleagues born in town. At ten, Mr. Essentialist meets a fellow lay preacher, but from a different religion. They want to do business, and so they strike a chord of lay preacher colleagues' sympathy. At eleven, he meets a foreign-looking woman he remembers seeing at his local "Clean the Streets" campaign. His normal unease with foreign-looking people gives way to the warmth of two fellow campaigners; and at twelve, he meets Mr. Just S. Essentialist who is just like him, but who is essentialist about being a Free Mason, too. The two don't hit it off. At each of these times, even Mr. Essentialist is negotiating two crosscutting cleavages: class versus region, religion versus faith as such, phenotype versus neighborhood commitment, sameness and suspicion—in other words, identity and difference. If this is a normal morning's worth of multiple identities, then multiculturalists should insist on a more interesting challenge. Multiculturalism is not about absolute cultural differences because crosscutting identities are omnipresent even for the essentialist. It is, instead, about a proactive awareness of these crosscutting cultural cleavages and a culture concept to deal with them.

The trouble is thus not so much with Mr. Essentialist himself, for he at least knows when to cut across so-called absolute difference; rather, the trouble is with the guy who writes books about him, Professor I. M. Norm, Chair of Essentialist Social Science. It is he who keeps reproducing the stale social science that cannot see how pluri-identic the "simple essentialists" are. What prevents these social scientists from seeing the flexibility that is all around them is their own narrow vision of culture. If it were right to regard some reified culture as the limit of anyone else's horizons and as the determining force behind everyone's actions, then urban life as we know it would be sociologically unthinkable and behaviorally impossible. It would be like Galileo measuring out the expanding universe but insisting that Rome had been dumped right in the middle of it. No competent analysis of social life can pretend to be surprised at the crosscutting nature of cultural identifications. Rather, it must wonder why people, including researchers themselves, so often talk and act as if things were simpler than they are, or even were in Nietzsche's times. Yet the essentialist view of culture cannot be written off as mere rubbish; precisely because so many people espouse it, it forms our chief analytical problem.

One reason why culture, whether national, ethnic, or religious, can still appear as an absolute is that each of these claims is repeated in very predictable contexts. We fight wars and watch Olympic games as nationals, we fight discrimination as ethnics, and contest moral issues as members of religious, or antireligious, communities. It is precisely when these neat separations clash that the absolute nature of one or another reified culture is questioned: when religious groups raise objections to the laws or policies of their nation-state, when spokespeople for an ethnic group call for secession from the state on religious grounds, or when nationalists declare ethnic or religious dissent to be treason. It is then that the differentiated cultural claims are pitched against each other. The most common arguments are then about the dividing lines between the public sphere and the private, between freedom of expression and the state monopoly on coercive force, and between democratic legitimacy and the rights of minoritized groups. It will be noted that it is always the (usually self-appointed) elites in all three cultural fields who keep attempting to refix the dividing lines.

A second reason why all three essentialized visions of culture retain their semblance of objectively given identities lies in their function to argue for rights. People refer to nationality to promote their rights of civic equality, they refer to religious cultures to reclaim their freedom of conscience and their right to moral dissent, and they invoke ethnic cultures to protest against discrimination or demand affirmative action. To essentialize one or another of these cultures is a useful strategy in arguing for rights and exemptions, collective demands, and even group privileges. Yet the essentialist view of culture creates more problems than it resolves, and one must say this clearly as a student of the social sciences.

Analytically speaking, the essentialist philosophy of culture cannot explain why cultures ever change or why, in fact, all cultures we know change all the time. Essentialists will often even fail to notice when they do. It is for these reasons that so many anthropologists have recently renewed their consensus against an essentialist view of culture.[1] American anthropologists Catherine Lutz and Lila Abu-Lughod (1990) have even suggested to scrap the word culture from the vocabulary of social scientists altogether because of its current misuse in public rhetoric: "For many [now], . . . the term [culture] seems to connote . . . coherence, uniformity and timelessness in the meaning systems of a given group, and to operate rather like the earlier concept of 'race' in identifying fundamentally different, essentialized, and homogenized social units. . . . [It then] falsely fixes the boundaries between groups in an absolute and artificial way" (p. 9).

Yet we cannot ban words; and even if we replace the word "culture" with the word "discourse," we will still mean much the same thing and thus contend with the same problem. We need to rethink the word rather than throw it away. This is a political imperative, too, since to reduce people's culture to their nationality, ethnicity, or religion is an intrinsically normative act. Even when it claims to liberate people, it is deep-down authoritarian. While it cannot be disowned or written off, it needs to be challenged by, and among, those who work for the multicultural project.

The most subtle and relevant of these challenges has been formulated by Chicago anthropologist Terence Turner (1993). He distinguishes a good social science of culture from a bad one, and likewise a good multiculturalism from a bad one. They stand and fall on the same criterion: whether they essentialize culture. Difference multiculturalism, the bad variety, removes cultural phenomena from their social, political, and economic flexibility; it freezes them into stable, usually ethnic, traits; and it thus fetishizes all so-called cultural boundaries. Outside these boundaries, it assumes the rhetoric of cultural relativism: Every group has its own moral universe, and every person is locked into the universe of his or her group. Inside the boundaries, it assumes the power to formulate binding rules and canons for all. How unliberating it is can be seen from its focus on elites and its preoccupation with conformity. In its focus on elites, it is a form of cultural imperialism in reverse: It is not Their group, but Our group that invented civilization, developed the first maths and sciences, wrote the greatest literature, discovered everyone else, and found out the ultimate truths. To take an example that Turner does not name, one may think of Martin Bernal's (1987) well-publicized argument in *Black Athena: The Afroasiatic Roots of Classical Civilization*. The ancient Greeks, Bernal claims, acquired their civilization from repeated invasions by Western Asians and by Egyptians, whom he claims were black Africans. The creation of the dominant Western version of "high culture" was thus based on theft, and subsequent denial of theft, of black African culture. The empirical evidence (Bernal 1987, 1991) is, to

88

say the least, a matter of very serious doubt (Lefkowitz and Rogers 1996; Lefkowitz 1996), but this is not even the point we need to make here. Rather, a rewriting of history such as Bernal's is as ethnocentric as Eurocentrism itself, and equally elitist in its view of what culture is about. It is not about daily living and individual choices, but about grand past achievements, ideas of "high culture" as opposed to "low," and about the ethnic pride that the "high and mighty" are supposed to engender. Those who do not share this pride, or indeed this view of culture, can be written off as "bad" members of the group, and they can even be excluded as outsiders. At this point, difference multiculturalism turns into an instrument of repression rather than liberation.

The best formulation of what happens that I have heard is not from a social scientist, but from my brother Ralf Baumann, a medic who observed it on the women's ward of a Berlin hospital: "A ghetto from the inside is a totalitarian state." It matters little, then, whose ghetto it is: whether it is cultural nationalists who exclude others as "ethnics," religious elites who exclude doubters as "heretics and apostates," or Afrocentric leaders who exclude dissenters as "coconuts: brown on the outside, but white within." All these strategies are repressive, and the multiculturalism that they produce will be the sole property of those elites that abuse their power to define the world as others should see it.

What a critical multiculturalism might ask questions about is far less ethnicist, exclusivist, and elitist in its assumptions, and Turner (1993) elaborates the point lucidly. Given that we know beyond any doubt that culture is not the product of some evolution from the primitive to the refined, what do we mean by such terms as civilization, the advance of science and technology, great and ungreat literature, the morals and politics of discovering, and the so-called ultimate truths? A liberating theory of culture and multiculturalism is, first and foremost, a new theory and a new praxis of culture. Turner's distinctions make this abundantly clear, and we have in this book already made some progress toward the goal. We thus have the right starting points in hand. We are no longer content to view nation-states as if they had neither ethnic nor religious implications. Rather, they can be seen to be aiming at creating supertribes and developing civil religions and quasi-religious civic cultures. We no longer pretend that we, or for that matter anyone else, might know what the word "ethnic" could mean. Instead, we have seen ethnicity as a social construct that mistranslates relational difference into absolute and natural difference. We no longer believe that religions are a cultural baggage of unchanging truths and have recognized them as navigational systems that depend upon the user's position in historical time and political space. We can now sharpen our focus on the two theories of culture that are at stake, and we can see how they relate to each other. We have distinguished two theories of culture. One of them, the essentialist, is popular in the media and in much political rhetoric, both about minorities and among them. The other, the processual theory, is far less popular, but it is the only theory that can be of use both to students of the social sciences and to committed multiculturalists.

So far, the matter sounds like a choice between a false but popular theory of culture and a scientifically productive but unpopular one. It would be quite wrong, however, to leave it at that, and there are two compelling reasons why the matter is not one of a choice between two opposing theories. The first reason lies in the golden rule of every empirical social scientist: Informants are never wrong; they have reasons to think what they think. In practice this means that we need to study their views until we comprehend the contexts of what they are saying. The essentialist theory is part of the realities that social scientists must examine and with which multiculturalists must engage. If the people we study come out with theories we find false, we cannot simply rubbish them as "false ideology" or "false consciousness." They form part of the realities we study, and we need to understand how they work, why people use them, and what people want to achieve with them. Very often, what they want to achieve is a sense of cultural continuity, a firm sense of cultural oneness or identity, and a stronger claim to community rights. It is not the social scientist's job to discredit these aims, but to understand why and under what conditions people use an essentialist theory to achieve their aims. This is the chief reason why the popular essentialist theory of culture needs to be taken seriously: It partly shapes the realities we need to understand.

In understanding these realities, however, we will find something quite surprising: The same people who often profess the essentialist theory of culture will, in many of their actions, use the processual theory of culture. Consider, for instance, the following case. A man or woman with great leadership skills wants to strengthen the sense of solidarity and unity among a group of followers. What he or she must do is convince them of the unity of their culture and portray this unity as a heritage from the past. In the past, it will be said, this heritage of unity was dormant: It was there but was not recognized. In the present, it will be said, this dormant heritage of unity is woken up to become real and powerful, fulfilling and liberating. To convince the followers that this great historic awakening is credible, the leader needs to preach an essentialist theory of culture: "Our group will act and will be, and deep down always has been, united in its thinking and identity." Yet employing this essentialist rhetoric is in fact a creative act. The leader propagates a unity that, empirically, has never been there in the past. The rhetoric is essentialist, yet the activity is processual. Culture is said, by such a leader, to be rooted in an unchangeable past, yet the leader can only hope to create it *because* he or she knows culture to be malleable and pliable, open to change and new consciousness. What the culture-forging leader preaches is the essentialist theory; what he or she practices is the processual theory. What such leaders call ancient cultural differences are, in fact, conscious acts of differentiation, and what they call essential identities are, in fact, processual identifications. All "having" of culture is a making of culture, yet all making of culture will be portrayed as an act of reconfirming an already existing potential.

The two theories are thus not opposites. Rather, the processual theory is implicit in all essentialist rhetoric. To visualize the point, one may think of all kinds of culture-shaping leaders: from the most conservative-sounding revivalists of a national or ethnic or religious unity, dim in the past but blazing bright for the future, to the most revolutionary-sounding forgers of a new cultural unity that fulfills the neglected potentials of an unjust historical past. The same dialectic applies, whether we think of fundamentalist leaders who "re"-invent an orthodoxy that never existed or of rousing prophetic revolutionaries who rally for massive change in the name of a tradition that has lain dormant and needs now to be fulfilled. From Ayatollah Khomeini on the conservative side to Louis Farrakhan on the revolutionary side, the dialectic is the same throughout: Those who preach an essentialist theory of culture rely upon the accuracy of the processual theory of culture. If that were not the way culture worked, how could anyone even hope to bring about cultural change?

So far, the dialectic is simple. Yet what about people who are not gifted with the skills of mass leadership? They, after all, are the majority in all kinds of groups, and they are the ones whom the leaders lead into essentialist understandings of culture. As so often in the social sciences, the greatest sophistication is found among those who seem, to the thoughtless observer, the least sophisticated. What I wish to argue is, in short, that perfectly unexceptional people can be observed to command a double discursive competence when it comes to their theories about culture, and they develop this dual discursive competence more strongly the more they expose themselves to everyday multicultural practice. What, then, is meant by this double, or dual, discursive competence?

As we have seen, the two theories of culture are not two equal alternatives, with one to be rubbished as false and the other to be hammered home as correct. Things would be simple if that were the case, but alas, it is not. This gives us a problem of language when we use the word "theory." All of us are shaped by the natural sciences view that two opposite theories cannot both be correct. You cannot maintain that the earth is flat and also say it is round. You cannot even maintain that the flat earth theory is a subtheory of the round earth theory, as we have done in saying that the essentialist theory of culture implies the processual theory of culture. We thus need to get away from using the word "theory" in describing the two understandings. Gratefully, there is indeed a better word we can use. We can regard the two theories of culture as two discourses about and of culture. By discourse, we mean a way of talking in speech and, just as importantly, a way of social action. The best analysis of the term is contained in the previously mentioned book on emotions written by American anthropologists Catherine Lutz and Lila Abu-Lughod (1990). Of the many uses of the word "discourse," we may stress two in particular. One focuses the analysis of language and action on pragmatics, rather than semantics. In other words, one deals not with unchangeable semantic meanings buried deep down in what people say and do, but with understanding what they say and do in regard to their practical intentions. The second use of the word "discourse" relates these "large-scale pragmatics" to the structures of power with which people must deal (Lutz and Abu-Lughod 1990, 9–10).

Using these two leads, we will find it easier to do justice to both theories of culture—the essentialist, partial one and the processual, comprehensive one—if we call them, not theories, but discourses of culture. The point I wish to make about double or dual discursive competence is now very straightforward: Most people practice a double discursive competence when it comes to their discourses about culture, and they develop this dual discursive competence more strongly the more they expose themselves to multicultural practices. In some situations, they can speak of, or treat, their own culture or somebody else's as if it were the tied and tagged baggage of a national, ethnic, or religious group. They can thus essentialize their discourse of culture to the point of creating totally static stereotypes, and they can do this to the culture they regard as their own just as easily as they do it to cultures they regard as alien. In other situations, however, they can speak of, and treat, their own culture or somebody else's as if it were plastic and pliable, something that is to be shaped rather than has been shaped, something you make rather than have.

We thus cannot advance a multicultural understanding of culture if we treat the essentialist view and the processual view as two opposite theories and call one of them true and the other one false. The result would be the supreme arrogance of a supremely mad social scientist, as if the people we studied were schizophrenics who maintain that the earth is flat as well as round. We have a lot to gain as soon as we theorize what people say and do about culture as two discourses, both of them rational in their different contexts. It opens up a whole new universe of study. By viewing culture as the object of two discursive competences, one essentialist and one processual, we can study and appreciate the culture-making sophistication of exactly those people who are usually treated as the dupes of "their" reified cultures.

This turn to seeing culture as a double discursive construction has immediate political implications. It is, I submit, a liberating cultural-political tool. We can get away from seeing people as the victims of their own or someone else's reifications and can begin to study how they are, in fact, the architects of the multicultural future.

We have made enormous theoretical headway in this brief chapter. Let me try to summarize it. There is an essentialist discourse of culture, which is applied both to minorities and among them. We cannot rubbish it as wrong, because the very people we need to understand use it, too. There is a processual discourse of culture, which is more useful to social scientists but is also used by some leaders and most grassroots minority groups. Both discourses have their purposes. One of them serves the reification of culture, which is wanted by majority media, majority politicians, many minority leaders, and, for instance, parents who wish to give their children a sense of cultural belonging and identity. The other discourse serves the processual remaking of culture, which is wanted by all those who, in one situation or another, want to escape from the stereotyping of the reifying discourse. Culture is thus not the tied and tagged baggage that belongs with one national, ethnic, or religious group, nor is it some spur-of-the-moment improvization without roots or rules. Culture is two things at once, that is, a dual discursive construction. It is the conservative "re"-construction of a reified essence at one moment, and the pathfinding new construction of a processual agency at the next moment. It vacillates between the two poles, and therein lies the sophistication and dialectial beauty of the concept. Yet in the end, all the comforts of having a culture rely upon remaking that culture, and the dominant discourse of culture as an unchangeable heritage is only a conservative-sounding subcomponent of the processual truth: All the culture to be had is culture in the making, all cultural differences are acts of differentiation, and all cultural identities are acts of cultural identification. At the same time, we must take care not to rule out of court the genuine views of the people whose lives we try to understand. There may not be a lot of logic to viewing culture as an entity or identity fixed once for all times. But there is a great logic to needing that partial truth as well. It is hard to emancipate children, let alone people deprived of equal civil rights, without enculturating them into a cultural identity: "This is what We do, and that is Our culture; and that is what They do, so that is Theirs." The people we try to understand are never wrong just because we disagree. On the contrary, we must, and as we shall see in chapter 10, can credit them with a capacity to deal with a multicultural sophistication that social scientists have been slow to recognize. This is the hopeful news. Let us now face the trouble of doing two things at once: recognizing that cultural essentialism is widespread and understandable, and demanding that it is not the sole basis for social scientists to understand the nature of culture.

Can the multicultural riddle be solved by encompassing this discursive nature of culture? That must be the question for a committed multiculturalist as well as for a student of the social sciences. If multiculturalism is a new understanding of culture as a dialectical and discursive process, we will want to cross-examine multicultural theory in that light. To do so fairly, we start the next two chapters, not with pointed or historical quotations, but with full-length citations from sources we want to critique and go beyond.

Notes

1. Up-to-date analyses and rejections of cultural essentialism have been worked out most compellingly in the ethnographic writings of Avtar Brah (1987), Thomas Eriksen (1988), Bruce Kapferer (1988), and Ann Phoenix (1988); they have been enshrined as a renewed consensus by such leading theoreticians as Barth (1994b), Keesing (1994), Sahlins (1994), Vayda (1994), van der Veer (1995), and Vertovec (1995).

Further Reading

Turner, Terence. 1993. "Anthropology and Multiculturalism: What Is Anthropology that Multiculturalists Should Be Mindful of It?" *Cultural Anthropology* 8 (4): 411–29.

Baumann, Gerd. 1997. "Dominant and Demotic Discourses of Culture: Their Relevance to Multi-Ethnic Alliances." Pp. 209–25 in *Debating Cultural Hybridity: Multi-Cultural Identities and the Politics of Racism*, eds. P. Werbner and T. Modood. London: Zed Books.

8

Multicultural Theory, I:
The Sales Talk and the Small Print

Are You Same Enough to Be Equal?

It is fairly common to refer to people as living in, or belonging to, a particular culture. However, this is too simple. . . . It is equally true that individuals can be members of many different cultural groups and have multiple group identities. (Verma 1990, 45)

The core of the emerging model of cultural pluralism in most Western societies is that the different ethnic, cultural, linguistic and religious groups making up society ought to have equal access to power or economic or political resources. (Verma 1990, 49)

The central point to be kept in mind is the necessity for ethnic and cultural minority groups to be able to participate in some of the institutions of the nation state as a whole. Also, their children ought to be able to accept the core values, attitudes and concepts that support the development of such a national identity framework. (Verma 1990, 51)

THE PURPOSE OF THIS CHAPTER is not to sort out one good theory of multiculturalism from so many bad ones. Rather, it is to develop and rehearse some common standards applicable to all theoretical pronouncements. "The most important thing about reading," so my best teacher told me, "is developing your own crap detector." This has two advantages at once. To exercise critical reading means not only to appreciate what is good about the worst sources but also to train the eye for the shortcomings and aporias hidden between the lines of the best. The skill of reading between the lines can then be applied to any other sources, too, and this wider applicability is all the more useful since multicultural theorizing is an industry undergoing phenomenal growth.[1] As with any spiraling branch of literature, the only practical way is to work out some basic criteria that can be applied to the good, the bad, and the indifferent alike. Although the literature is still in flux, the criteria to be used here can be defined sharply enough. They must correspond to the new understanding of culture that we have worked out in the previous chapter.

The particular sources I have chosen range from the world-famous to the local or parochial, and this is quite as it should be: No one knows all the answers simply because they live in Metropolis rather than Middletown, or because they are paid by a university rather than a mosque. They also range from the theoretically self-conscious to the unconsciously theoretical. This again is quite as it should be, for most of the social theory we encounter does not come dressed up in the robes of grand theory, but dressed down in the humble smock of how readers "should" think to "help" in practical matters. This is, after all, how people buy other things, too: The sales talk warms their hearts, and the theoretical small print is taken on trust—until the Pay Later bills are marked Now Due. In investing in multiculturalism, we cannot buy the sales talk without reading the small print, too, and this is the point of this chapter. For all the offers we shall examine, the criteria will be the same: Do they essentialize such ideas as the nation-state, ethnic identity, religion, or even culture in general, or do they go beyond such reified absolutes? If they do, can they come up with tangible ideas, or do they end up in a dreamy haze? To put it briefly: Are they pluralist without being vague?

The most pluralist view of multiculturalism can also be the practically vaguest view, and one example for many may be taken from Britain. Gajendra Verma (1990) approaches the multicultural future with the boundless inclusivism that many people would expect from a Hindu philosopher: At root, all reality is plural, and only the necessities of living together, that is, the accidents of history, have divided one culture, society, and ethnicity from the other. It is even recognized as "true that individuals can be members of many different cultural groups" (pp. 45–46). On the pluralism scale, Verma thus scores at the very top. Yet it is precisely these "cultural groups" that, according to Verma, "make up society" (pp. 54–56). Modern pluralist society with its multitude of crosscutting cleavages is thus portrayed as an aggregate of quasi-corporate groups, much as colonial anthropologists like Radcliffe-Brown (1924) saw tribal societies made up of corporate clans bound together by a "culture" of blood and clan (see Kuper 1977). With one lapse of analytical thinking, we are thus back to viewing a modern society of crisscrossing intersections, as if it were some patchwork quilt of different colors or faiths, all definable by themselves and operating one without reference to the other. The only pluralism that Verma can thus wish for is that of the nation-state "co-ordinating the goals of each cultural group" (p. 48) as if they were one people, "but allowing each to maintain its culture" (p. 48) as if that culture were fixed once for all. Yet this nation-state of ethnic or religious ghettos is to give all cultural "groups equal access to power" (p. 49). Two questions arise: Why should it be the nation-state as we know it, a supertribal and quasi-religious enterprise, to which we look for ethnic or religious equality, and what exactly is meant by equality?

The first question is brushed under the carpet because the author has not analyzed the hyphen in nation-state. He wants to see multicultural "diversity within the framework of national identity" (p. 51). This means that everyone must "accept the core values" that support national ideologies. One must wonder how realistic this is. Are Muslims in Britain to accept the British blasphemy law that protects the Christian faith but no other? Or is that not "core" enough when it comes to Salman Rushdie's *The Satanic Verses?* The second question is circumvented by the vague demand that "the different ethnic and religious groups making up society have equal power in terms of access to economic and political resources" (p. 50). This sounds fine at first reading, but again, what does it mean? Does it mean equality of opportunity by providing the same education for all youth, perhaps regardless of their parents' cultural loyalties or mother tongues? Does it mean equality of employment rates, and thus a lifelong administration of work vouchers that are based on "where" one comes from or "belongs"? Who determines where one comes from and where exactly one is meant to belong? Who is to add up these roots, and on what criteria? The answers remain unclear, not because Verma lacks in good intentions or even pluralist sensitivity, but because he has not fully thought through the implications of the pluralist nature of modern society, even within the boundaries of the once-modern nation-state.

From the pluralist but inconclusive, let us turn to the meaningful, which is, however, exclusivist in the extreme. Choosing an example that can be replicated in many countries of the West, let us analyze *The Muslim Guide for Teachers, Employers, Community Workers and Social Administrators* (McDermott and Ahsan 1979). The book is meant to be read by all who deal with Muslim citizens, not only in Britain but also in continental Europe and the United States (p. 8). Most of it concerns what Muslims must do to be good Muslims, followed by a list of resources, services, and exemptions that they must be given to achieve that end. At first sight, there is nothing wrong with this: Who would not approve of Muslims being good Muslims, and who would begrudge anyone the resources and exemptions that are needed to be a good Muslim wherever one lives? Of course one needs *halaal* meals at school, in the hospital, and in prison. But what does it mean, and who will determine what it entails to be a good Muslim? The *Muslim Guide* is therefore not wrong in its intentions of facts; it *is* wrong, however, in the multicultural theory that its various sponsors have smuggled in under the guise of the *Foreword*, by a British commissioner; the second *Foreword*, by a mosque official; and the *Authors' Preface*. It is in these added bits, the bits that piggyback on the main text, that the theory can be found, and this hidden theory is misleading, I contend, on several counts of pluralist thinking.

Let us start with the first. From the desk of the Chairman of the British Commission for Racial Equality, we read: "Islam is a way of life, with firm and clear views on a variety of issues such as hygiene, diet, education, the role of women and, indeed, life after death. The daily lives of Muslims, their manners and mores are all determined by these views" (McDermott and Ahsan 1979, 5). Describing the views of all Muslims, from New York to Baghdad, as "determined" by "Muslim" traditions and views, the good chairman, paid by the British government to "advance the integration of Muslims," has failed to distinguish between the different ways of people who "wish to practise their religion and preserve their cultural identity" (p. 7). All of these people's cultural identities, which, in Britain alone, range from West Africa to East Asia and from northern China to South Asia, have been squeezed tight and compressed into one: A Muslim is a Muslim, whatever else he or she may be. The logic of such an argument is clear: Since the only difference that counts is the difference of religion, it is "Islam as such" that needs multiculturalist awareness from schools and hospitals, social workers and prisons. So simple is life for a state-appointed multiculturalist manager. I must admit that, reading the text, I am always reminded of a person I knew, a frightened mullah protecting his village flock from the evils of pluralism that he saw sweeping across the rural Sudan. This parallel is unfair, of course, because the guardian of other people's orthodoxy does use the sacred multiculturalist mantra "diversity and pluralism" (p. 8). Yet this diversity and pluralism are never applied to the Muslim flock themselves; they are only ever used to reproach non-Muslims of their lack of love for the diversity and pluralism that Muslims are supposed to have imported into British public life. Could not a Muslim, too, respect and appreciate the diversity and pluralism of fellow Muslims, wherever they are from?

By way of a thought experiment, let us turn the tables for a moment. What would a preface read like if it recognized the diversity and pluralism with which Muslims shape and endow their lives in a not-yet-multicultural culture? Would Muslims not be emancipated from the monocultural life-form of being Muslim to becoming differentiated, pluralist, and meaning-rich participants in a multicultural society? One would hope so, but even the authors of the *The Muslim Guide* persist in painting Muslim men, women, and youths as photocopies of a never-changing canon of rules:

> The belief in God permeates every walk of a Muslim's life and finds expression in every cultural or social practice, whether it be the etiquette of everyday life, the modes of human inter-relationships, the modes of eating and dressing . . . sleeping or even driving a car. (McDermott and Ahsan 1979, 17)

I wonder how many alternative traffic codes we will need in a society that treats Muslim drivers as Muslims first. Need we print everyone's religious identity on their driving licenses, too, as happens with Ahmediyya Muslims who want a passport in Pakistan? Satire aside, the matter is serious when it comes to a theory of multiculturalism that is based on such an overbearingly normative view of religion as a person's one determining identity. One may shudder at the pressures of conformity and obedience that this view could justify in the face of internal opposition or "members" who do not pull the party line. Under such a regime of difference "multi"-culturalism, what would happen to the rights of all those Muslims who do not practice their religion? In most of the literature this is a taboo subject, but there are two exceptions at least. Thijl Sunier, the most up-to-date scholar of Muslims in the Netherlands, suggested a cautious estimate that some 40 percent of Muslims could not be considered "practising Muslims" (Sunier 1995, 200 n.3). Remy Leveau, the most experienced historian of Muslims in France, puts his estimate at about a third and points to a most surprising paradox: "[T]he *rigorous* interpretation of Islam among *intellectual* believers appears to be a strategy for coping with French society" (Leveau 1988, 112; italics mine). It is the nonpracticing Muslims, often of an intellectual and/or politically activist bent, who invoke Islamic principles in their most fundamentalist form to make them serve particularist ethnic or universally pan-Arabist political programs (pp. 112–29). The paradox is entirely plausible, for religion, with its aura of immutable truths, does act as a trump card to raise the odds in any other matter of contention. We have said as much in chapter 2. But be that as it may, both Sunier (1995) and Leveau (1988) have moved us a long distance away from our "multi"-cultural state-appointed manager who claims that "the daily lives of Muslims . . . are all determined" by Islam (McDermott and Ahsan 1979, 5). Good intentions not withstanding, such pronouncements can endorse the most repressive impositions of power, and we shall encounter the same point again in our next example.

Having reviewed a multiculturalist vision uncritical of the nation-state and another seemingly multiculturalist one that reduces people's culture to their religion at birth, let us turn to the third reification that must be overcome: the reduction of people's culture to their ethnic identity. The sharpest and also the most courageous critique of ethnic absolutism can be found in the writings of the London theorist of "black culture" in Britain, Paul Gilroy. What struck Gilroy in the late 1980s was an unsettling convergence between the antiracist political left and the racist far right of British politics: Both of them had come to see culture as if it were an ethnic heirloom or a straightjacket with which people were born. Their otherwise unbridgeable differences aside, both parties saw "cultures supposedly sealed from one another forever by ethnic lines" (Gilroy 1987, 55). A few years later, Gilroy identified their shared "belief in the absolute nature of ethnic categories [which was] . . . compounded firstly by a reductive conception of culture and secondly by a culturalist conception of race and ethnic identity" (Gilroy 1992, 50). In other words, one camp reduced culture to "race"; the other camp declared ethnic identity to be the sole determinant of culture. This surprising complementarity between minority advocates and minority bashers was and is leading to "new forms of racism [which] . . . are distinguished by the extent to which they identify race with the terms 'culture' and 'identity'" (Gilroy 1992, 53). There are two social consequences to such an absolutist fallacy. The first stands in parallel to the Muslim case of cultural absolutism. The people who are labeled Muslim will be subjected to "culture policing" from within: Are you Muslim enough to get Muslim rights? The people who are labeled black, are asked: Are you *really* black, or are you a coconut, dark on the outside, but white within? If you are found wanting in conformity to your leaders' norms, then not only do you deserve no community rights but also you are a blemish on the community body itself. The second consequence is more pronounced in the ethnic case than it was in the Muslim case: It is the expectation from outsiders that you conform to your own community's rules. A student of mine put this dilemma in the form of a fake application. She imagined a state authority asking an applicant to certify her cultural conformity to qualify for the adequate multicultural treatment:

Q. 17: Eligibility for Multicultural Equality (form EME 1)

Have you been certified: [ ] national enough
                             [ ] religious enough
                             [ ] ethnic enough

to be equal?

TICK ONLY ACCORDING TO THE CERTIFICATES YOU
RECEIVED.

Name: _____ Date: _____
Stamps of the Certifying Authorities: 1:
                                           2:
                                           3:

This problem, too, has been tackled in a more serious form by
the Chicago anthropologist Terence Turner, whose work we
have already discussed. Regarding the situation in the United
States, Turner observed that, in its internally nonpluralist forms,

> *multiculturalism* tends to become a form of identity politics,
> in which the concept of culture becomes merged with that of
> ethnic identity. From an anthropological standpoint, this
> move, at least in its more simplistic ideological forms, is
> fraught with dangers both theoretical and practical. It risks
> essentializing the idea of culture as the property of an ethnic
> group or race; it risks reifying cultures as separate entities by
> overemphasizing their boundedness and mutual distinctness;
> it risks overemphasizing the internal homogeneity of cultures
> in terms that potentially legitimize repressive demands for
> communal conformity. (Turner 1993, 411–12; italics original)

The danger applies as much to an ethnicist reduction of culture as it does to a religionist and a nationalist view of culture,
and Turner affirms the multicultural necessity of constantly
"challenging, revising, and relativizing basic notions and principles *common* to dominant and minority cultures alike, so as to

construct a more vital, open, and democratic *common* culture" (Turner 1993, 412; italics original). We shall return to this in the next chapter; for the moment, it is worth remembering that communalist versions of culture, whether they are based on nationality, religion, or ethnicity, demand communalist conformity. This is not what a multiculturalist can want, whether it is enforced from the inside or from the outside.

Where, then, is the solution that gives due recognition to cultural diversity outside and yet safeguards due pluralism within these boundaries? This is the question asked by probably the most influential, and easily the most erudite, contribution to the multicultural debate to date. In the next chapter I therefore highlight the theory of multiculturalism advanced by Canadian philosopher Charles Taylor.

Notes

1. As is characteristic of such a spiraling industry, the literature of multiculturalism comprises mainly edited volumes, rather than works in which any one author tries to move matters forward comprehensively. Of the many recent collections, some deserve mention here: Donald and Rattansi (1992); Glick Schiller et al. (1992); Goldberg (1994); Kymlicka (1995); Rex and Drury (1994); and van Steenbergen (1994). As always with such brick-sized collections, they contain contributions of widely varying quality. Some of the best ones are mentioned in later chapters.

Further Reading

Gilroy, Paul. 1992. "The End of Antiracism." Pp. 49–61 in *"Race," Culture and Difference*, eds. J. Donald and A. Rattansi. London: Sage.

9

Multicultural Theory, II:
The Values and the Valid

What Is It Prof. Taylor Should "Recognize"?

> [I]n the nature of the case, there is no such thing as [an] inward
> generation [of identity], monologically understood. In order to
> understand the close connection between identity and recog-
> nition, we have to take into acount a crucial feature of the
> human condition. . . . This feature of human life is its funda-
> mentally *dialogical* character. . . . We define our identity
> always in dialogue with, sometimes in struggle against, the
> things our significant others want to see in us. . . . [T]he mak-
> ing and sustaining of our identity . . . remains dialogical
> throughout our lives. Thus my discovering my own identity
> doesn't mean that I work it out in isolation, but that I negoti-
> ate it through dialogue, partly overt, partly internal, with
> others. (Taylor 1994, 32–34)

THIS FINE PASSAGE of understanding identity theory is taken from
the Canadian philosopher Charles Taylor's much acclaimed book
Multiculturalism: Examining the Politics of Recognition ([1992]
1994). As the title makes clear, Taylor views multiculturalism as
a problem of "recognition," and half of his famous short treatise,
no longer than fifty pages in all, is devoted to finding out how the

issue of cultural recognition arose in the first place. The philosopher traces the eighteenth- and nineteenth-century shifts in European elite thinking that allowed the demand for "recognition" of one's "cultural identity" to become the chief agenda of twentieth-century multiculturalism. With the decline of the predemocratic rank-based social orders, a new significance has been awarded to ideas and ideals of equal personal dignity and cultural or subcultural authenticity. This shift, however, opens up a serious problem, and this forms the second part of the essay: How can we award the same universal recognition to an ever-widening variety of mutually exclusive designs of authenticity and identity, especially when these involve a politics of (stressing) difference? This politics of difference may well be necessary to demand recognition, but it must simultaneously deny that there is any one cultural value that is truly universal. Even the value of recognition, let alone tolerance or mere coexistence, must then appear as culturally biased in the best case, or as culturally self-serving or hegemonic in the worst. Taylor has identified this dilemma of multiculturalism, or to be precise this dilemma of recognition, at a very high level of abstract thinking. At this level, however, there appears to be no answer. Even at the end of his intellectual tour de force, Taylor returns to a frustratingly elusive compromise:

> There must be something midway between the inauthentic and homogenizing demand for recognition of equal worth [for all cultures] on the one hand, and the self-immurement within ethnocentric standards, on the other. There are other cultures, and we have to live together more and more, both on a world scale and commingled in each individual society.
>
> What there is is the presumption of equal worth I described above: a stance we take in embarking on the study of the other. . . . How can this presumption be grounded? One ground that has been proposed in a religious one. . . . I can't rule out such a view. But merely on the human level, one

could argue that it is reasonable to suppose that cultures that have provided the horizon of meaning . . . over a long period of time . . . are almost certain to have something that deserves our admiration and respect, even if it is accompanied by much that we have to abhor and reject. . . . It is only arrogance, or some analogous moral failing, that can deprive us of this. But what the presumption requires of us is not peremptory and inauthentic judgements of equal value, but a willingness to be open to comparative cultural study. (Taylor 1994, 72–73)

The passage sounds eminently reasonable at first sight. We cannot bury our ethnocentric heads in the traditional values of our own reified culture, but neither can we recognize indiscriminately that any culture is as good as any other. We cannot outlaw cannibalism or racism and at the same time "recognize" the cannibal's or the racist's culture. To tackle this dilemma, the passage moves a fantastically long way in a few highly compressed sentences. Starting from wanting to recognize equal worth or value for all cultures, we get to the mere presumption of equal validity for a few selected cultures. We have reserved this presumption to long-established and widely recognized cultures only. There is thus no presumption of equal value that attaches to recent cultures, cultures deemed deviant by whomever has the power of such a judgment, and cultures that may arise tomorrow. This is not a million miles away from the nineteenth-century liberal who wants to "learn from other cultures," but only from certain cultures deemed worthy or ancient enough and who will only take to heart those lessons that suit his taste.

How can such a virtuoso essay have such a vague conclusion? The explanation, I contend, is that Taylor complicates the issue of recognition and simplifies the issue of culture. With the two mistakes reinforcing each other, the philosopher is reduced, at the end, to agonizing about an impossible blanket recognition for a nonexistent object. Let me start with the first point of critique.

The Multicultural Riddle

Taylor complicates the issue of recognition. The philosophical idea to equate multiculturalism with "the politics of recognition" was cautiously printed in quotation marks in the first edition of his essay; in the second edition, when the treatise was turned into a book, multiculturalism became *"the"* problem of the politics of recognition. Into this one term recognition, however, the philosopher has packed a truly staggering range of meanings: awareness, appreciation, respect or merely due respect, acceptance, and even admiration. With so many attitudes all conflated into one word of the author's own choice, the multicultural riddle has been complicated to a degree not hitherto known. It is no wonder that in the end, multiculturalism is "perhaps after all a moral issue" (1994, 73). This may be true, but if it is, then we must face two altogether different questions: Whose morals, and what do we mean by recognition?

Taylor has given a brilliant account of the shift in European philosophers' thinking that led them from seeking "honor" to seeking "recognition." He has thus unearthed the "roots" of a particular, and peculiarly Western, philosophical shift. But whose philosophers are these, and whose opinions are they meant to have shifted? Is there any evidence that all minorities demand the same kind of recognition across the board, be it the one à la Rousseau or the one à la Kant? Every likelihood speaks against it. Even in Taylor's own country, Canada, the demands for recognition that are made by Québecois, indigenous Inuit, and Asian (as opposed to Middle Eastern) Muslims differ widely in their political scope, philosophical arguments, and assumptions about culture. If the philosopher has shown one thing beyond doubt in his tracing of Western philosophies, it is this: The elites of each culture always put together their own visions of what they think multiculturalism is about. That someone can find an English-language word called "recognition" under which all these visions can be lumped together as if ultimately they meant the same thing is a great feat of abstract competence. But does this competence amount to an objective act of synthesis? It clearly does not, and it cannot, as Taylor's original problem makes clear:

> The charge I'm thinking of here is provoked by the claim sometimes made on behalf of "difference-blind" liberalism that it can offer a neutral ground on which people of all cultures can meet and coexist. . . . Liberalism [however] is not a possible meeting ground for all cultures, but is the political expression of one range of cultures, and quite incompatible with other ranges. Moreover, as many Muslims are well aware, Western liberalism is not so much an expression of the secular, postreligious outlook that happens to be popular among liberal *intellectuals* as a more organic outgrowth of Christianity. . . . All this is to say that liberalism can't and shouldn't claim complete cultural neutrality. Liberalism is also a fighting creed. (Taylor 1994, 62; italics in original)

To argue that Rousseau's or Kant's view of "recognition" is what all these cultures out there are really on about is to argue precisely what the philosopher has ruled out from the start—that some hegemonic idea of justice or value acts as the unbiased referee amid the multicultural fray. The philosopher's dilemma is far superior, of course, to the thick-headed ethnocentrism of an old-fashioned Western cultural imperialism that maintained that "other cultures" were worse. Yet it can appear as cultural imperialism at one philosophical remove. It is the superior reading of eighteenth-century Western philosophers that tells us the two things we need to understand about multiculturalism—first, that it is a politics of the same recognition for everyone, no matter how "they" see the problem, and second, that recognition can only be granted as a moral presumption of equal value, not as a recognition of equal validity. The latter contention may well be true, but the former is an assumption for which there is no empirical evidence.

The Multicultural Riddle

Let us turn to the second reason why Taylor's fallback position of "studying other cultures" will satisfy few multiculturalists. The cultures that Taylor deems worthy of the presumption of equal worth are specified as those "that have provided the horizon of meaning for *large* numbers of human beings, of diverse characters and temperaments, over a *long* period of time—that have, in other words, *articulated* their sense of the good, the holy, the admirable" (1994, 72; italics mine). If we need such a list of criteria for the respectable cultures that are eligible for multicultural recognition, then who falls out? Do we also want a list of cultures that are too young, too small scale, too impure and hybrid, or too inarticulate to deserve "recognition" in its two dozen conflated meanings? The philosopher Taylor's narrow concept of culture is even more problematic than his carry-all concept of recognition.

To see this problem, let us turn to the middle section of his treatise. Just when it becomes clear that "the" problem of multiculturalism, recognition, cannot be answered in the abstract, the discussion seeks direction from an empirical battle. Living in Quebec, Taylor focuses on the rights to recognition of the French-speaking Canadians of Quebec, whose political and cultural leaders have demanded a wide variety of measures to ensure this recognition. At the most radical end, these measures demand an independent state of Quebec; even at the moderate end, they deny the choice of English-language schooling to all youths from French-speaking and even from overseas backgrounds, and they legally force businesses with more than fifty employees to be run in French. The rationale for such restrictive and culturally repressive laws is what Quebec nationalists call "survival" or "cultural survival." By this fake-biological euphemism they mean the continued dominance of the French language and Québecois ways of doing things. Taylor, an Anglophone working in Quebec, is aware of the problem:

Multicultural Theory, II: The Values and the Valid

> Policies aimed at survival actively seek to *create* members of the community, for instance, in their assuring that future generations continue to identify as French-speakers. There is no way that these policies could be seen as just providing a facility to already existing people. Quebeckers, therefore, and those who give similar importance to this kind of collective goal, tend to opt for a rather different model of a liberal society. . . . Here are two imcompatible views of liberal society. (Taylor 1994, 58–60)

To speak of "two incompatible views of liberal society" when pitching Canadian Anglophone pan-nationalism against its greatest foe, Québecois secessionism, is a stroke of genius worthy of a Francophone diplomat such as Talleyrand. Taylor's readers need have no opinion on what counts as liberal; they may well have opinions, however, on what cultural nationalists mean by "survival." We have already consulted Handler's (1988) ethnography of Québecois cultural nationalism in chapter 3. His detailed empirical analysis has shown up the strategic machinations and the discursive tricks that Quebec nationalists employ to essentialize a national-cultural identity of Québecois. They are the same that we have found in other ethnopolitical nationalist movements (McDonald 1989; Heiberg 1989): All of these movements are led, not by the "common people" for whom they claim to speak, but by thoroughly urbanized and often university-educated politicians and practical fixers. These culturalist avant-gardes play on people's confusions between better social planning for the future and a putatively "natural" order from the past. Their ideologies treat so-called blood bonds as if they were bonds of conviction, and they treat soil, their favorite code word for both state sovereignty and national citizenship, as if it were subject to blood bonds. All these blood-and-soil strategies help turn flexible and situational cultural identifications into hard-and-fast cultural nationalisms. The cultural-nationalist identity manufactured in this way is always exclusive and bounded, and it is often modeled on the quasi-religious claims that we have already reviewed in chapters 3 and 4. It is one thing to speak of the "survival" needs of selected "old" cultures which claim that there are "two incompatible views of liberal society" (Taylor 1994, 60). It is quite another thing to observe how politicians play the game of "ethnopolitics [which] . . . ideologizes, reifies, modifies, and sometimes virtually re-creates the putatively distinctive and unique cultural heritages" of a particular nationalist constituency (Rothschild 1981, 2–3). In the case of Quebec, for example, it is hard to see what is liberal about forcing English-speaking parents migrating from India to Canada to send their children to be schooled in French in Quebec. The question, whenever one cultural party speaks of "survival," is simple enough: Survival of what, and doom for whom?

What is meant to "survive" in Taylor's chosen example is the Québecois culture, or whatever their leaders recognize as such. Yet does this end hallow all means, and what does the end mean in the first place? What does it imply to say that a "culture" must either "survive" or "die"? Our deliberations on the culture concept, worked out in the previous chapter, have already warned us of this biologistical view that paints culture as if it were some superhuman "body that lives and dies . . . like a living organism" (Clifford 1988, 235). This may well be a "useful fiction" (Rosaldo 1989, 217) for cultural nationalists to put about, but the fiction is dangerous in several ways. It treats culture as an exclusive club that one either is, or is not, a full "member" of; it makes cultural boundaries appear hermetic, instead of fluid and pliable according to the context and to people's own agency; and it favors the ascendancy of the *"real*-culture watchdogs" who police the cultural purity and social conformity of the less powerful people whom they count as "their members" and treat as their subordinates.

With this, we come to the crux of Taylor's text. We have reviewed two problems, namely, that too much variety was telescoped into the imperiously Western concept of "recognition" and that the text treats some cultures as undeserving of the presumption of equal worth and allows others to enforce that presumption by punitive laws and the forced assimilation of unwilling minorities. What is at stake, therefore, is again the key question of multiculturalism: What is culture?

The ways in which one can update Taylor's culture concept are laid out most clearly by Ghanaian-American philosopher of African American studies Anthony Appiah. Appiah's (1994) critique charges Taylor's treatise with a blind spot that is very common in multicultural theorizing: "[O]ne reasonable ground for suspicion of much contemporary multicultural talk is that it presupposes conceptions of collective identity that are remarkably unsubtle in their understandings of the processes by which identities, both individual and collective, develop" (Appiah 1994, 156). One could add as a footnote here that identities do not actually "develop" by themselves all that often; rather, they are developed, that is, they are postulated, asserted, and then filled with prescriptive norms by people with interests. Multiculturalism is thus not merely a question of letting a thousand flowers bloom and making sure that no single species gets an unfair advantage. It is also a question of critical thinking: Who declares what into a flower, and what artificial processes of selection, fertilization, and resource manipulation have gone into its development? As Appiah hints, Taylor commits the same mistake as the Quebec nationalists themselves: Just because there are people who identify and have the power to reify a "Quebec culture," they therefore take the right to establish a Quebeco-cultural "society." When Taylor speaks of "the survival of certain 'societies,'" Appiah points out, "[Taylor] means groups whose continuity through time consists in the transmission through the generations of a certain culture, of distinctive institutions, values, and practices" (1994, 157).

To treat culture as if it were the same as society is one of the oldest problems in the social sciences. In colonial anthropology, it led straight to the tribalist fallacy that equated one culture with one self-enclosed population: the very opposite of what a multiculturalist can want. In colonial practice, it led straight to the imposition of "plural" social orders, as opposed to pluralist, economic, social, and political orders. The outsider scholar who first recognized these processes of divide and rule has remained justly famous ever since (Furnivall 1939, 1948). He diagnosed societies, or rather racist regimes, where each "ethnic culture" was seduced, by the colonial masters, to run its own social system without regard for the others. From there to apartheid was a very small step. Are we to repeat this conflation of culture and society in a Western nation-state where all kinds of cultural cleavages cut right across one another and where the very essence of any cultural identity lies in its dialogical character with others? It is hard to imagine Charles Taylor entertaining any delusion as anachronistic and dangerous as that. Yet his desire to credit cultural nationalists in Quebec with being "liberal" (1994, 59–61) brings him close to exactly that position. Why should the most lucid theorist of identity as a dialogical process fall into such a rusty nineteenth-century trap? The reason is simple, and it goes much deeper than the case of Quebec. Since Taylor identifies multiculturalism as a problem of "recognition" in its two dozen different senses, the question must be: recognition of what? Taylor's answer must be: recognition, in all conceivable senses, of fixed "cultural identities." These cultural identities, moreover, are supposed to be ancient and continuous, proven and integral, and determining of people's entire horizons.

When all is said and done, Taylor's treatise should be called not *The Politics of Recognition*, but *Recognizing Cultures*. It treats recognition as a complicated and multifaceted thing, yet treats cultural identity as a simple and one-dimensional thing. Forgotten are the pages where he stressed that contemporary cultural identities are irreducibly dialogical. It was as a mark of recognition that I placed them at the beginning of this chapter, although they are actually tucked away in the middle of Taylor's review (pp. 32–34). People, Taylor observed, come to identify themselves, not in a soliloquy, but in dialogue with others. Multiculturalists must do the same, and so must cultural nationalists wherever they are— not because this is a finer way to deal with identity, but because it is the only possible way to even think of identity. Yet one could rip these pages out of Taylor's book, and no first-time reader would ever notice their absence. The insight has failed to influence the philosopher's text as it could have.[1]

If multiculturalism is indeed a "politics of recognition," as Taylor says, what then is it that is to be recognized? Is it one of those reified "cultures," perhaps that of the local majority whose leaders are most adept at essentializing its norms for survival? Or should we recognize cultural diversity, that is, the commitment of citizens and residents to recognize the dialogical nature of all their identities? If multiculturalism is about recognizing one culture, or even two or ten as they are, then I have no further interest in it. A hegemony of ten is better than a hegemony of one, but the first thing about recognizing any culture is to recognize culture for what it is: not an imposition of fixed and normed identites, but a dialogical process of making sense with and through others. These others will, in time, become part of your own multicultural culture, as Taylor knows well on the personal level: "If some of the things I most value are accessible to me only in relation to the person I love, then she becomes part of my identity" (p. 34). Like all of Taylor's short moments of recognizing the dialogical nature of all identity, this sentence, too, reduces world-historical problems to the level of methodological individualism.[2] It sounds like the engineer from Iceland who once told me: "My wife is from Thailand; so I now have two cultures."

It is for these reasons that Appiah (1994) asks Taylor to complicate the second part of his equation, too. Having complicated the issue of recognition to the nth philosophical degree, why do we have to apply it to a vision of culture that is as dead as a dodo, and twice as essentialist as General de Gaulle in Quebec? One can, of course, wind the clock back to some nineteenth-century idea of fixed identities within one or another version of cultural nationalism, and there is no law against ignoring Nietzsche or even fifty years of research on ethnicity and its reifications. Yet Taylor's own argument would benefit vastly more from a vision of a multicultural Quebec that looks one step ahead, rather than two steps back: "[W]e need to go on to the next necessary step, which is to ask whether the identities constructed in this way are ones we . . . can be happy with in the longer run. . . . I think (and Taylor, I gather, does not) that the desire of some Québecois to require people who are 'ethnically' francophone to teach their children in French steps over a boundary. I believe . . . that this is, in some sense, the same boundary that is crossed by someone who demands that I organize my life around my 'race' or my sexuality. . . . Between the politics of recognition and the politics of compulsion, there is no bright line" (Appiah 1994, 162–63). Where there is no bright line between two outdated extremes, there usually gapes a gray border zone patrolled by the culture police from one side or the other. It is there that the recognition of one reified culture must degenerate into, and may even enforce, the compulsion of other people's cultures, which, in the process of being policed, get reified, too.

We have asked of Taylor's text what it is that multiculturalists should "recognize" and have suggested two answers. One, which Taylor alludes to but does not make enough of, is the dialogical nature of all identities, or rather, identifications. Multicultural society is not a patchwork of five or ten fixed cultural identities, but an elastic web of crosscutting and always mutually situational, identifications. Secondly, if we think of culture as a discursive process, rather than an inventory of rules, we can avoid the bleak corner into which Taylor has argued himself, namely, the blind alley where we must select which cultural values can be recognized as valid and which can be rejected. The task is not only impossible, as Taylor himself has found out, but also is wrongly conceived, as Appiah has shown. What needs to be recognized, therefore, is not one reified culture as opposed to another one. Rather, it is the dialogical nature of all identities and, consequently, that different cultural identifications can and will, in a multicultural society, cut across each other's reified boundaries. If these theoretical suggestions are to be of use, then they should be tested on the empirical evidence. Let us see, therefore, how they can shed light on current multicultural practices and perhaps even illuminate good multicultural praxis.

Notes

1. One can only speculate about the reasons why this key insight is given so little importance. Taylor bases his arguments on Bakhtin ([1929] 1984), who developed his insight into the dialogical nature of identity through a literary critique of Dostoyevsky's novels. To Bakhtin, it was clear that Dostoyevsky's characters were not simply individuals put alongside each other in Russia, but exemplars of trying to be human within a society. Yet Taylor's analysis of what was shown by Bakhtin (never mind Dostoyevsky) screws the great social insight back to the level of little isolated individuals. Not one of Taylor's sentences about the dialogical nature of identity goes beyond the biologistic reference points of having two parents and a spouse. If this were all there is to dialogical identity, we might as well have a separate cultural identity for every nuclear family, hallowed by its own religion and language if necessary. This cannot be Taylor's intention, and his false turning may have more to do with the old philosophical habit of "methodological individualism."

2. Methodological individualism is the trade name for a fallacy that is common even in the social sciences. Its fault is that it treats mass-scale social phenomena as if they were only larger-scale blow-ups of individual phenomena. It argues as if, say, the racism prevalent in a whole nation-state were merely the sum of individual citizens' racisms projected onto a larger screen. This pushes out of sight the most inter-

esting social factor, namely, the invention of a larger screen. How can so many individual racists establish one particular racist use of the language in general, or of job adverts or interview procedures in particular? The same is true of other inequalities: One cannot, methodologically, reduce the unequal treatment of women or gays or the homeless to the individual prejudices of men or heterosexuals or homeowners. It is to draw attention to this missing link that Emile Durkheim (1947) invented the term "social fact" when studying the seemingly most individual act, that of suicide (Durkheim ([1893] 1947). While it is true that all social agency is performed by individual human beings, we need to study the transmissions of individual errors into established social faults to get to the bottom of social discrimination. In theoretical terms, it may well be true that all social actions are performed by individuals. That is why the fallacy of individualism is a "methodological" fallacy only. Yet at the same time, every human being takes shape as a social being, and ultimately, therefore, there is no such thing as truly individual behavior: Even a martyr is a martyr only through others. Whatever we do, we do in a dialogue with "meaningful others" (Mead 1934). The handiest phrase was coined by the late John Blacking (1972), who took as his motto a Venda proverb from South Africa: "Man is man through fellow man" in whatever he or she does—and thus becomes. It is for this reason, the social dependence of humans on others, that individualism, which may or may not be a theoretical good, can be a methodological fallacy in the social study of humans.

Further Reading

Taylor, Charles. 1994. "The Politics of Recognition." Pp. 25–74 in *Multiculturalism. Examining the Politics of Recognition*, ed. A. Gutmann. Princeton, NJ: Princeton University Press.

Appiah, K. Anthony. 1994. "Identity, Authenticity, Survival: Multicultural Societies and Social Reproduction." Pp. 149–64 in *Multiculturalism. Examining the Politics of Recognition*, ed. A. Gutmann. Princeton, NJ: Princeton University Press.

10

Multicultural Praxis: The Banal and the Best

From Culti-Parading to Multi-Relating

Q: So that [multifaith worship at school] doesn't bother you?

Hursh: No; all religions say the same few things.

Q: Really? What do they say? Can you—

Hursh: They say: God exists. And he is the creator. And secondly, be good; and then if you are good, you'll have it good, either while you're alive or maybe later.

Q: But don't they mean different things when they say God is the Creator?

Hursh: Well yes, God has a different character in each [religion]. . . .

Q: But doesn't this interfaith produce a mish-mash of religions?

Hursh: I suppose it does. But I find that—quite sensible, really.
(conversation with Hursh Joshi (17), then a
student at a school in Southall, London, 1991).

The Multicultural Riddle

THE FORM OF MULTICULTURALISM that most people are most familiar with in the West is probably the organized representation of cultural difference. Its favorite genre and emblem is the multiethnic parade, that is, a kind of stage show that, in its own jargon, "celebrates diversity." Observing this kind of practice as a "Canadian institution," Audrey Kobayashi (1993, 206) has coined the expression "'red boots' multiculturalism" which typically consists of "folk dancing, cultural festivals and ethnic restaurants." The headlines are well known from almost any newspaper one chances to pick up: New Yorkers of fifty-two cultures join the Mayor's Parade; Londoners of sixteen cultures enjoyed an evening of Chinese dancing; representatives of five cultures discussed the issue of women's rights in Middletown. There is nothing wrong with such ventures; yet they represent not so much a pluralist multiculturalism as a difference "multi"-culturalism that parades the distinctiveness of each so-called cultural group and remains in thrall to each reified understanding of culture. Instead of breaking down cultural barriers, which is its chief claim, it has to reinscribe these cultural borders and fix them as if they were given by nature.

To advance from this cultish parading of "cultures" to a more dialogical understanding of multicultural praxis, I suggest we devote this whole chapter to one multicultural city. This is because we need to understand the daily and the small-scale multicultural routines to find the difference between the banal and the best, and no multicultural city has been studied from more different angles than Southall, the "Little India" of London, England. Social science research in Southall has been able, over the past fifteen years, to move across all the ethnic and cultural boundaries that are so often taken at face value elsewhere, and this allows us a comprehensive view of multicultural possibilities and limitations alike.[1]

Southall is a town, or so its people call it, of some 66,000 people situated between London's Heathrow Airport and the western suburbs of the capital. In its central areas, more than half the population are Sikhs from India and East Africa; some 15 percent each are Hindus from India and Muslims from Pakistan; and the remainder are, in order of number, native English, Irish, and Afro-Caribbean by origin. Yet such an enumeration is a very misleading affair, as it masks the most crucial characteristic of Southall: the multitude of cleavages that cut across the categories we have just used. Such crosscutting cleavages can be, for instance, East African-Asian, an identification that cuts across the divide between Sikhs, Hindus, and Muslims; Roman Catholic, which cuts across the divide between Irish, Afro-Caribbean, and South Asian; or Punjabi-speaking, which separates some Hindus from others, some Muslims from others, and some Christians from others. Aside from these specifically local crosscutting cleavages, there are, of course, a number of others well known throughout Western cities: class identifications; political and residential identifications; and gendered, generational, and lifestyle identifications. What we thus find is not a patchwork of five or even fifty fixed cultures, one defineable without reference to the other, but precisely that elastic crisscrossing web of situational identifications that our considerations of theory have demanded already.

Even in such an environment of shifting identifications, we do still find the difference "multi"-culturalism described by Terence Turner. Apart from a certain amount of "red boots" or "multi-culti" parading, the most serious of these is what may be called community competition in the political field. This phenomenon reflects the peculiar way in which the British political system conceives the welfare of so-called immigrant communities. Rather than thinking in terms of civil rights and a culture-transcending equal treatment for all, the system encourages the representation and public servicing of minorities that can organize themselves to prove their cultural distinctiveness. We have outlined this system in chapter 4, which was devoted to civil cultures, and the process of turning migrants into pseudocorporate "communities" has been described in a number of cases (Morris 1968; Kalka 1991; Baumann 1996, 20–31, 59–71; Baumann 1997). In Southall, too, the fact that public resources are, as the word goes, targeted at cultural communities leads to a local political scene in which the common good is seen as a competition of any one community with any other community. The most memorable comment I have ever heard about this political system, which some call divide and rule, came from an African Caribbean musician in Southall. Observing how all the local politicians kept playing one community's needs against some other community's needs, he summarized the wasteful internecine effort with a physical image: "We're tied to each other, back to back, and struggling for fuck's sake to get freedom." In the process, every minority has to struggle against all others, and each of them becomes a community of disappointment and suspicion that complains that some other community is getting a better deal while the common good gets nowhere.

Yet in sharp contrast to these consequences of the reifying discourse in the political field, Southallians have gone far, in other fields, to engage the processual discourse of culture. In this dialogical praxis, no community and no culture can be defined without reference to the others, and multicultural praxis is not concerned with distinctiveness but with multirelational thinking. The test of such multirelational thinking can be put in the simple form of a question: "Do we regard the so-called others as a necessary part of who we are?" The question will turn out to be less simple than it looks, but we will come to that a page or two later. Let us first look at two examples how "the others" can indeed be incorporated into what "we" are and what "we" want.

My first example comes from the person who spoke of being "tied, back to back, and struggling for fuck's sake to get freedom." His great ambition was to get practice rooms and recording studios for Southall's young musicians. These come from different communities, and the normal way would have been to campaign for a music center in the name of Afro-Caribbeans, in the name of Asians, or in the name of some other cultural group. This is what the reifying discourse of Southall politics demands. Yet what this musician really wanted was a new kind of music based on a new kind of politics: a cross-cultural creative resource center called Southall Music Fusion. The point, to him, of being a musician in Southall was to fuse the different musics of Southallians into a Southallian music. The efforts continue, but one thing is clear: A Southall musician who campaigns for the creation of a shared Southallian music is engaged in a multiculturalism based on multirelational thinking.

Another example seems to be negative at first sight. Anglicanism is the state church of England and the nation-state religion whose official "Defender" is the Queen herself. Yet in Southall, where most Anglicans are not English by birth and most citizens are not Christian, even Anglicans cannot operate thoughtlessly. In 1989, St. George's Church, an Anglican congregation made up of equal parts English, Pakistani, and Afro-Caribbean members, was preparing its traditional Good Friday procession on Southall's streets. Yet tellingly, the procession was cancelled that year: Some members of the congregation declined to take part because, they observed, there were serious misgivings about some Sikh religious processions, and their public observance might now be misunderstood as a "white" or "Christian" or "Anglican" claim to "own the streets" of town as if they had more rights than Sikhs. Here again is an example of how multicultural thinking is multirelational thinking: The so-called "others" form a necessary part of what "we" think we are and want. One can easily think of other public processions and parades to see how advanced this kind of multicultural thinking is.[2] It makes perfect sense not only on the local level but also on the level of social theory: The ritual of the procession would take on a new meaning in a new context, and authentic as it was, its own community decided to scrap it.

Moral advancement, however, is not what this multirelational thinking needs to be about. Laudable as these two initiatives were, most Southallians prefer other means to chart the future of their multicultural society. The question stands unaltered: Do you regard the so-called other as a necessary part of who you are and what you want? Have you understood, better than Taylor, that all identity is dialogical? Many Southallians have. Within each of the reified communities of culture, there are moves at hand that integrate "outsiders." They take different forms in different communities, and the differences and details have been described and analyzed in the literature.[3] What is of most general interest here is a new kind of process that advances multicultural praxis where it happens and furthers multicultural thinking in our analysis. This is the process of multicultural convergence.

By the word convergence, a mathematician means that two or more vectors come to point in the same direction. Each of them seeks the same point of agreement; but each of them does so from its own point of origin and by its own route. Applied to the dynamics of culture, this is a truly multicultural process. We are no longer faced with one arrow that imitates the trajectory of some other arrow, as if some so-called minority were imitating one self-proclaimed majority. Nor are we faced with the processes called adjustment, acculturation, or integration in the sociological literature. What is observable here is something far more multirelational. What the word convergence describes are separate processes of cultural change pointing all in the same direction, but each taking a different path toward the same common point, the point of concurrence. To picture a simple example, most people who read this book will be wearing jeans. Jeans are an American, perhaps originally Genuese, piece of clothing. Most prople across the West have come to converge on jeans as the thing to wear when reading, laboring, or relaxing. Each of us wears the same thing, but this does not turn us all into Americans, or for that matter Genuese. There is no denying that the convergence on jeans reflects a North American hegemony in how we think of leisure wear or work gear. Yet there remain many subtle differences in how people of different backgrounds and lifestyles use and think of jeans. Students may get married in them, accountants will not; in London, you may wear them to the opera, in Amsterdam, they get you banned from second-rate discos. In the process of convergence, the different cultural vectors aim at the same point of convergence, but each keeps following it own logic.

A second remarkable feature about convergence is that the point of concurrence need not be defined by a hegemonic majority. The street styles of "hip" male teenagers in European cities are largely defined by the street styles defined among young African Americans in New York. Similarly, the 1980s fashion of men wearing earrings originated in a gay culture that tried to challenge masculine stereotypes. Needless to say, "Ice T." has gone warm by now and most gay men have given up earrings, but the recent historical insight remains productive: There is a plethora of separate paths toward a common point, and this common point need not be associated with a hegemonic majority. This is convergence; now look at Southall. We will find some processes of convergence that are planned, and others that proceed inadvertently.

An example of planned convergence has been mentioned already in referring to the project of a Southall Music Fusion. The idea was to create a style of musical crossover that cross-fertilized different stylistic traditions from Afro-Caribbean, South Asian, and white Southallians. There are innumerable other examples of planned convergence in the political field. In fact, wherever Southallians come together on a solidarity that cuts across ethnic, religious, or national distinctions, such as trade unions and political parties, neighborhood initiatives or voluntary associations, women's groups, gay groups, or civil rights campaigns, one may speak of processes of planned convergence.

The Multicultural Riddle

As the examples make clear once more, convergence processes need not strive after some point of concurrence defined by a hegemonic majority. The same applies to the unplanned and inadvertent processes of convergence.

Just as Southall people of many different backgrounds come to wear American-style jeans and favor the same Australian soap operas broadcast on British TV (Gillespie 1995), so inadvertent convergences proceed also in the less commercialized realms of everyday life. The first convergence that may strike an American tourist in Southall is what I called "the Southall gait": a particular way of walking cultivated by young men of all backgrounds that rang a bell with almost every Southall girl I ever asked about it. Its hegemonic model, they agreed, was a particular bodily habitus that had African American associations and used templates known from American TV programs to assert a particular "don't . . . with me" masculinity. The most astonishing convergence I found in Southall is a multicultural creation called "the Southall cousin." This concerns a convergence of all Southall's male youths upon invoking and claiming cousin bonds, many of them fictional, to get out of scrapes, claim large family networks, avoid fights, and disarm strict parents (Baumann 1995c). This convergence of cousin bonds followed Sikh, rather than Hindu, British, Irish, or Afro-Caribbean conventions, but youths of these latter backgrounds showed it just as much. I mention both these examples to stress that convergence processes can be truly multicultural: One cannot know in advance which majority or minority is the hegemonic force in any one case. Even two hegemonic forces can be at work at the same time.

The languages that Southallians speak have come to develop into two common dialects, one an identifiably West London accent of English, the other a mixture of Punjabi, Urdu, and Hindi that is recognized as *Southalli* by anyone who has heard the languages spoken on the Indian subcontinent. *Southalli* works on a mixed vocabulary and softens the clear consonantal contours that Southallians associate with a *pindhu* or "village" pronunciation. No less inadvertently, Southallians have come to converge on the celebration of children's birthdays in virtually all families, including those who, traditionally or even twenty years ago, did not celebrate individual birthdays at all. Children who see their school friends of different backgrounds being spoiled with birthday gifts once a year are an irresistible cultural force. Moreover, entering the domains of religious ritual, there is hardly a Sikh or Hindu home where families fail to celebrate Christmas. Almost all of them find that they have to give in to their children's wish to join the "English" rituals of posting Christmas cards and putting up a decorated Christmas tree, singing songs of Santa and reindeer, and feasting on an, often vegetarian, adaptation of Christmas dinner. These kinds of convergence can be interpreted as an evil piece of white cultural imperialism (Alibhai 1987), or they can be interpreted as a challenge to the so-called Durkheimian theory of ritual. Let us pause for a moment to consider the implications.

Concerning ritual, the classic social science theory is ascribed to Emile Durkheim, the founder of the modern sociology of religion. What Durkheim is supposed to have said is that the purpose of a society's rituals is for that society to celebrate its own existence. One may call this the Golden Calf Theory: When the Israelites danced around the Golden Calf, the new divinity they fashioned while Moses had left them for a meeting on Mount Sinai, they really danced around their collective identity as a group. In the words of Edmund Leach, one of the century's most eminent social scientists, "we engage in rituals in order to transmit collective messages to ourselves" (1976, 45). This is also the favorite theory of the "red boots" multiculturalists: In ritual, they say, we find the most authentic and sacred expression of people's national, ethnic, or religious identities. Yet the evidence from Southall seems to contradict this view: People celebrate rituals that are not traditionally their own, and there are many rituals, in fact, that are concerned with relationships to others, rather than with relationships within the ritual or cultural community. Do we then have to discard Durkheim's classic theory of ritual? Gratefully, we do not; rather, what we have to discard is a misreading of Durkheim that has found its way into every textbook I know. If the Golden Calf Theory of ritual is Durkheimian, then Durkheim was an anti-Durkheimian. Despite the dozens of books that have copied this mireading from other books, Durkheim never said the rubbish attributed to him. When he suggested that ritual expresses the identity of a society, he warned the reader by means of a Socratic question: "Is it the real society, such as it is and acts before our very eyes?" ([1915] 1971, 420). The answer is no: "[S]ociety is not an empirical fact, definite and observable"; it is something "in which [people] have never *really* lived. It is merely an idea" (1971, 420). Durkheim's theory is meant, also by him, to apply to a completely abstract quality that he called society, something that nowadays we call sociality or sociability and that is far removed from any reifiable community or culture in the narrow sense.

Let us test this multicultural insight one step further. Durkheim's theorem about ritual is also widely misread as "the Durkheimian theory of religion." This reading again makes nonsense of Durkheim and, empirically speaking, nonsense of Southall. In chapter 6, we followed Schiffauer's argument in refuting the unwarranted claim that religion was immutable baggage, either of truths or of falsehoods. We have replaced it with the analytical metaphor that every religion is a sextant—an instrument of orientation in uncharted waters, but also such a precision instrument that it measures all things in relation to its user's position in historical time and space. The evidence from Southall is as clear as Schiffauer's evidence from Germany: Religions change as people unpack them in new situations. In addition to these observations, we can trace processes of multicultural convergence even in the ways Southallians conceive of their religious truths.

Multicultural Praxis: The Banal and the Best

Examining religious practices, it is worth starting at a relatively mundane level. The worship in Sikh and Hindu temples has come to focus on a Sunday morning ritual performed by the whole congregation, a change of tradition that has also been observed in other parts of London (Vertovec 1992). This clearly reflects the hegemonic influence of British public culture, just as blue jeans reflected the hegemonic influence of American culture. A more important influence may be that of the linguistic convergence already alluded to. The language in which people explain their different religious ideas to each other is, more often than not, English, and this gives rise to commonplace glosses such as Sikhs calling the Ten Gurus "our gods" or, as commonly, "our prophets," and a Muslim *imam*, a Sikh *gyanni*, and a Hindu *pandit* all being referred to as "our priest" or "their priest." With regard to their injunctions, too, different religions are seen as permutations of a shared repertoire. Consider these explanations from young Southall people:

> The Muslims don't eat pork, and the Sikhs don't eat beef, and the Hindus don't eat meat at all.

> You see, the Muslims aren't allowed to drink, but they can smoke, and we [Sikhs] can't smoke but we can drink. So it's the same thing, only different, isn't it.

Such comparisons are expressed as commonplaces, but they are quite significant: They make religions appear not only comparable but even homologous, that is, built up of the same few elements common to all. Each of them can thus appear as one particular transformation of the same general structure. This shows a new habit of thinking of religious differences as relational, rather than absolute, and it is not far from here to a belief that all religions converge upon the same truth. Not only the young who have grown up in this incipiently multicultural environment, but even people in their seventies routinely come out with statements that "all religions are about the same truth" or even "about the same God."

This readiness to think of different religions converging upon a shared core of truth is widespread, but it does not mean, of course, that people cannot, in other contexts, lay claim to their own privileged position among other religions. As I said before, multirelational thinking need not be about moral merit. It is a way of arguing that questions the boundaries between reified cultures and attempts to turn absolute differences into relative differentiations. This does not mean that Southallians are at all times cosmopolitan liberals. As we argued in chapter 7 when we examined culture as a discursive process, the existence of a processual discourse does not mean the end of the reifying discourse. People need and use both, and in Southall's public life, religious differences can appear very stark and simplistic at times; it is a matter of context and situation whether people engage the reifying discourse of absolute differences or the processual discourse of relational differentiations.

In examining some processes of multicultural convergence, we have moved a good distance away from the banalities of "red boots" parading. We can see how people in a multicultural environment use both discourses of culture at the same time. In opting to use one or the other, the criteria are situational and pragmatic. There are goals one can only reach by reifying cultural difference. At the same time, there are goals for which one needs to get on with other people, and often this is best done by questioning and relativizing reified cultural boundaries. Southallians are not multicultural angels; but neither are they the dupes or clones of one cultural identity or another. To be a socially competent Southallian is to know when best to reify and when best to relativize difference. To understand multicultural praxis is to examine precisely when people shift from their one discourse to their other discourse. In studying these shifts, social scientists can make an enormous contribution to the multicultural future. The people we learn from by our research can show us the way from culti-parading to multi-relating, and we can show it to others. I shall return to the contribution that students of the social sciences can make in the final chapter, but it may be useful first to summarize the whole argument at a glance. I should add that this is one of several possible summaries. Other students of the social sciences may well have their own that lead to different conclusions.

Notes

1. The first among the recognized scholars who studied among the people of Southall were Avtar Brah (1987) and Parminder Bhachu (1985). This work was further broadened by some outstanding dissertations in sociology and anthropology (Hundleby 1987; Gillespie 1989; Larson 1989; Hawkes 1990; McGarry 1990; Yabsley 1990). More recently, Gillespie (1995) and Baumann (1996) have added two full-length ethnographies and a number of articles (listed in the References). The work is set to continue, as we shall see in chapter 12.

2. The demand to have processions, parades, or marches in public spaces is one of the key mechanisms to promote sectarianism and sabotage multicultural practice. Examples are found wherever things go wrong between communities identified by some reified culture. The most dramatic is Northern Ireland, where the Marching Season, due every summer, destroys whatever peace process has been started over the previous nine months. For a multicultural utopia à la Aristoteles or Thomas More, Francis Bacon or Thomas Paine, a good rule would be simple: "Unless you parade with enemies, lock yourself up at home."

3. All these processes involve questioning and disengaging the chief equation of the reifying discourse, namely, that culture must equal either ethnic or national or religious community. Among Sikhs, one could observe strong dynamics of forging new communities on a basis that combined differentiations of caste, migratory history, and perceptions of class. Hindu Southallians often expressed a claim to encompassing ideas and people of other communities. Muslim

The Multicultural Riddle

Southallians stressed that the local community of believers entailed a contending variety of cultures divided on criteria of language and migratory path, as well as ethnic and national loyalties. Among Afro-Caribbean Southallians, one could identify several approaches aimed at "finding," and thus consciously creating, a new culture. White Southallians, finally, have developed three fairly distinct strategies in response to their equivocal attitudes to the community and cultural identities ascribed to them. For a more detailed description, see Baumann (1996, 109–44, 190–92).

Further Reading

Baumann, Gerd. 1996. *Contesting Culture: Discourses of Identity in Multi-Ethnic London.* Cambridge: Cambridge University Press; esp. pp. 173–87.

11

From Dreaming to Meaning:
A Summary

Multiculturalism Is a New Understanding of Culture

Q: What is culture?

A: Habbits.

Q: What is tradition?

A: I think it means the way you do thinks.

Q: What is your culture?

A: . . . New things made that there haven't been made.
> (written replies to three questions from three
> twelve-year-old school students in Southall, London.)

OUR SEARCH FOR THE BASICS of multicultural thinking started out with the multicultural dream: an abiding vision of equality across all cultural differentiations. The question is how this equality might be achieved, and there are three conceptions of rights that are on offer. Human rights are the most inclusive and wide-ranging, yet they are also the least enforceable both within and across nation-states. Civil rights, the time-honored pledge of modern democracies, are easier to enforce, but they are usually limited to citizens, and they have a poor record of bridging inequalities based on national, ethnic, and religious histories of discrimination. Community rights have gained enormous ground over the past twenty years, but they, too, raise questions: Which kinds of communities should be recognized, how democratically are they run, and do we need to be ghettoized to get equal rights? All three kinds of rights deliver partial promises at best of fulfilling the multicultural dream. To turn from dreaming to meaning, we need to analyze the three components of the multicultural triangle: the nation-state and its national identity, the idea of ethnicity or ethnic identity, and the workings of religion and religious identity.

The nation-state claims a privileged position against both these other identities, ethnic and religious. It claims to be post-ethnic, replacing all ethnic bonds with bonds of rational association and ethnically blind equal provision. The first claim cannot stand up since all nation-states make use of pseudotribal ideologies, not to speak of ethnic discrimination, to prove their worth as imagined communities. The second claim is that of replacing religious community by a secular consensus on a religiously neutral common ground. Yet this common ground needs filling in by quasi-religious ideologies of civic culture, which amounts to each nation-state producing its own civil religion. The nation-state, the first corner of the multicultural triangle, is thus not simply the neutral arena within which the multicultural dream can be realized; rather, it is itself one of the problems. The ideas of ethnic identity and religious identity, however, need to be questioned in the same way.

Ethnic identity and its practical upshot, ethnopolitics, base their authority on bonds of blood and descent, and even the bonds of language and culture are treated as if they were natural facts. This essentialist position does not hold water: Far from being a natural identity, ethnicity is a carefully cultivated, and not seldom a manipulated, strategy of social action led by unelected elites who often exploit or mislead their supposed beneficiaries. Religion, on the other hand, provides no unchanging identities. While believers think of their faiths as unchanging, religions are more like highly context-sensitive sextants than like the tied and tagged baggage of unified groups.

None of the three analyses can destroy what they analyze. National identifications are going to remain for the foreseeable future, and partaking in national civic cultures is still the best way of securing equal rights for most people, but national identities cannot be accepted as postethnic or as nonreligious. Ethnic identifications are necessary to win long-standing battles over ethnic discrimination, but they cannot be accepted as given by nature, and they must constantly be checked for the influence of self-serving elites. Religious identifications will not go away and they may in fact be the most sensitive and creative identifications that people can find and reshape, but they need to be watched for the same reason as national and ethnic identifications: the influence of self-serving elites.

In replacing the word "identities" with the word "identifications," however, we have taken a liberating analytical step. We no longer see any identity as fixed beyond question and change. National identity is no longer as rationalist as it pretends to be, ethnic identity is no longer as natural as it appears to be, and religious identity is no longer as eternally unchanging as it is preached to be. All of them are identifications related to a reified understanding of culture. Multiculturalism is, therefore, a new understanding of culture. If we thought of culture as something we have and are members of, we can now think of culture as something we make and are shapers of. The essentialist understanding of culture (whether nationalist, ethnicist, or religiously orthodox) can be turned into a processual, and even discursive, understanding of culture. Culture is not a giant photocopy machine that turns out clones, but the most sensitive capacity of humans who cannot but produce change even when they mean to produce stability. To say the same thing in a new situation is to say another thing. All three cultural identities are thus processes of identification that turn out, in philosophical analysis as well as daily practice, to be dialogical: They result and get hardened, or they get used creatively and turn subtle, in the daily process of approaching so-called others. How then should we deal with cultural others?

The answers proposed by the theorists of multiculturalism should be scrutinized in the light of our three critiques, and there is a minimum requirement that all multicultural writing has to answer, whether it renders its theory of culture explicit or hides it between the lines. It must not reify national, ethnic, or religious identities. Rather, it must be aware that all identities are identifications in context and that they are thus situational and flexible, imaginative and innovative—even when they do not intend to be. Multiculturalism thus cannot be a question of: Are you national enough, ethnic enough, religious enough to be equal? This kind of equality is not worth dreaming about, and all the meaning it can have will lie in the power of self-elected elites. The same goes for multicultural theorizing that is done from the philosopher's point of view but treats identity as a reified cultural label, rather than a dialogical process. By reifying cultural identity one risks playing along with cultural essentialists, and one risks condoning the policing of cultural purity by elitist elites. If the dialogical nature of all identifications is taken seriously, however, we may hope to find some guidance in the multicultural realities as they can be observed empirically.

The best starting point for doing this is to rethink our idea of what culture is. Reified visions of culture are undoubtedly part of the social realities we study. National, ethnic, and religious minorities use them, and probably need them, some of the time. Simultaneously, however, we can discover a processual discourse of culture, that is, a theory of culture that understands differences as relational, rather than absolute. It recognizes that there are many different cleavages of identification and that these cleavages cut across each other. Instead of viewing society as a patchwork of five or fifty cultural groups, it views social life as an elastic and crisscrossing web of multiple identifications. People make choices whom to identify with when and where, and they even make choices when to engage the reifying discourse of culture and when to engage the processual discourse. We have thus progressed from a reified through a processual to a discursive understanding of culture. In looking for empirical examples, we can find the best evidence on the smallest scale.

An ethnographic study of multicultural realities as lived in one place can produce new clues that fill in the theoretical gap we have noticed: the gap between people claiming reified identities and their everyday necessity of crosscutting identifications. People who live in a multicultural milieu need to do both to reach their personal, family, or community goals. What develops in such an environment is a double discursive competence: People know when to reify one of their identities, and they know when to question their own reifications. What also develops are processes of multicultural convergence: the simultaneous reorientation of otherwise separate traditions upon a new point of cross-cultural agreement. That this point of agreement is attractive to all must mean that it has hegemonic force, but it need not belong to majorities alone. In studying how and when people field their reifications of culture, and how and when they put them to one side or even throw them to the winds, students of the social sciences play a crucial role. If multicultural dreaming is to turn into multicultural meaning, this double discursive understanding of culture needs to be searched out in practice.

This is all the more important since there is such a counterproductive gulf between our multicultural theorizing and our researching practice. The theoretical literature has embellished the word "citizenship" with a dozen new slogans in half-dozen years: That makes two new sorts of citizenship per year. Yet much of our empirical research keeps asking yesterday's questions and giving last year's answers. We will never know what an identity *is* unless we have tried to dissolve it into situational identifications; we will never learn what culture *is* until we understand it as a dialectic, that is, double discursive, process: People reify it and at the same time undo their reifications, we will never understand why identities are dialogical if we take a philosopher's family as our example. In other words, we need to find out empirically how exactly people manage to shape dialogical identities while at the same time reifying monological ones.

It would be wonderful if such research could give us a foolproof recipe for future action and empower us with one set of hard-and-fast rules to usher in the multicultural future without ever thinking again. Yet I must confess to some skepticism on that score. Speaking in general, I am not convinced that there is such a thing as "scientific action" in social life, that is, one way of acting that is scientifically sound and another way that can be proven scientifically wrong. There are more gaps than links between social studies and the dream of a value-neutral social "science" on the one hand and between social "science" and the bureaucrats' dream of social engineering on the other. What I feel obliged to do, however, is to indicate how writing this book has changed my views beyond the point of return. All identities are identifications, all identifications are dialogical, and all struggles for a common dream are practical. The last is the most important. What do I do to become a useful multicultural citizen, and how do I break through the reifications with which the multicultural dreamscape has been land mined? My personal answer is simple, and so I can put it in a footnote: It is no more than the personal opinion of one citizen who studies the social sciences.[1] What may be of more practical interest is to devote the final chapter to outlining some feasible research projects that other students of the multicultural riddle could find rewarding, too.

From Dreaming to Meaning: A Summary

Notes

1. If I had to formulate six rules for a multicultural future on the basis of multirelational thinking, I would phrase them like this: (1) We must recognize the modern nation-state as a problematic creation, both pseudoethnic and pseudosecular, that needs reforming. This may be why political theorists keep inventing new ideal qualifications of citizenship; (2) we need to rethink national, ethnic, and religious identities into processes, that is, we should recognize them as reified entities and then reform them by pulling apart their favorite reifications; (3) unless human rights will suddenly succeed, we may try to base our expectations of equality upon enforceable rights awarded on the basis of residence rights, rather than civic status. Medium-term residence, whether legal or illegal, must give rise to rights that are enforceable vis-à-vis nation-states, in the end perhaps through international law; (4) we will do well to encourage all commitments that cut across the established national, ethnic, or religious divides. Women's and gender rights, labor and environmental rights, the rights of children and prisoners are obvious points to cut across the tired old established divides; (5) we need to develop a less nationalist, ethnicist, or religiously exclusive social science, that gets us away from reifying the ghettoized communities we study and allows us to study their crosscutting bonds of exchange and solidarity; (6) we can make this progress possible by recognizing point (1), thinking point (2), and practicing points (3), (4), and (5). The best practice to develop multirelational, multicultural thinking is easy: Try to unreify all accepted reifications by finding crosscutting cleavages. Whenever the reifying discourse talks about citizens or aliens, purple or green ethnics, believers or atheists, ask about rich or poor citizens, powerful or manipulated ethnics, married or sexual-minority believers. Who are the minorities within majorities, who are the unseen majorities right across minorities? Combine every method of questioning to every possible category around you, for the permutations are endless when it comes to questioning reifications: Six questions invalidate thirty-six answers, and twelve invalidate twelve times twelve. The principle is always the same: Ask a question that cuts across the cleavage regarded as absolute in any one context. Nothing in social life is based on an absolute, not even the idea of what counts as a majority or even a cultural group.

12

From Meaning to Practice:
What Students Can Do

New Understandings Require New Projects

> "How can you contrive to write so even?" (Miss Bingley in Jane Austen, 1813, *Pride and Prejudice*, chap. 10)

> "I have nothing to do to-day. My practice is never very absorbing." (Dr. Watson in Arthur Conan Doyle, 1892, *The Adventures of Sherlock Holmes:* "The Red-Headed League")

> "It has long been an axiom of mine that the little things are infinitely the most important." (Sherlock Holmes in Arthur Conan Doyle, 1892, *The Adventures of Sherlock Holmes:* "A Case of Identity")

IF WE WANT TO REFORM multicultural practice, let us begin with our own practice as students of the social sciences. Research on the multicultural riddle has tended to fall apart into two large heaps: the grand theoretical work that asks us to rethink everything on the basis of no serious empirical data and the empirical work that keeps churning out the same banalities as it did twenty years ago. An example for the theoretical heap is the avalanche of calls to rethink the idea of citizenship. In the space of six years, social scientists have managed to come up with more than a dozen calls to rethink citizenship: "differentiated citizenship" (Young 1989), "postnational citizenship" (Soysal 1994), "neo-republican citizenship" (van Gunsteren 1994), "cultural citizenship" (Turner 1994), "multicultural citizenship" (Kymlicka 1995), "transnational citizenship" (Bauböck 1995)—the list of new adjectives can be continued, and no doubt it will be. What all these new slogans are aimed at doing is extending the classic idea of social citizenship championed by political scientist Thomas Marshall (1965) and exploring new meanings of participating in the processes of public decision making. This is all as it should be: Theoreticians, too, have to live. The only question is: What can any of these slogans mean in real life? The clearest answers I have found come from the political scientist Iris Marion Young (1990), but even these are not exactly precise: "[W]e require participatory structures in which actual people, with their geographical, ethnic, gender and occupational differences, assert their perspectives on social issues within institutions that encourage the representation of their distinct voices" (p. 116).

Closing one's eyes to imagine such a participatory structure, one might see a neighborhood meeting in which everyone speaks as someone particular at any one moment: black or white, Christian or Muslim, man or woman, gay or straight, rich or poor. I have attended some such meetings in Southall and found that in most cases it was one particular group that took over the meeting: sometimes the loudest, sometimes the best organized, sometimes simply the majority. But then, Young reminds us, we should not think of these identity groups as stable at all: "In complex, highly differentiated societies like our own, all persons have multiple group identifications [because even] . . . individual persons as constituted partly by their group affinities and relations cannot be unified, [for they] themselves are heterogeneous and not necessarily constant" (Young 1990, 48).

From Meaning to Practice: What Students Can Do

Closing one's eyes once more, one may now have to imagine an endless ocean where a thousand swimmers' heads pop up in unpredictable places and all of them whisper "differentiated citizenship" at one time or another. True, they all seem to converge at least on the slogan, but where in this pluralist but vague ocean is the participatory structure? One would have to do empirical work to find out.

Those social scientists who work empirically, on the other hand, keep hammering home the inadequacies and injustices entailed in citizenship and nationality as controlled by nation-state elites, describe participatory structures that do not work, or unmask routines that work on the basis of exclusion, inequality, and selfish sectionalism. As their theoretical colleagues invent new words without reality, the empirical students describe the same old realities, time and again in the same words. The former observe nothing and question everything, the latter observe everything and question nothing. The same division is even more apparent in studies of ethnicity. In their theoretical introductions, many studies of ethnicity quote Stuart Hall's vision of multiple identities, such as the following, which could be read as a free-floating angel's definition of cultural infinity: "It is the politics of recognizing that all of us are composed of multiple social identities, not one. That we are all complexly constructed through different categories, of different antagonisms, and these may have the effect of locating us socially in multiple positions of marginality and subordination, but which do not operate on us in exactly the same way" (Hall 1991, 57).

One cannot but admire such a vision of complexity; yet when it comes to empirical studies of ethnicity, most students are still given topics such as "The Turks in Berlin," "The Berbers in Paris," or "The Sikhs in New York." The focus is on a national, ethnic, or religious minority as if anyone could know in advance how this minority is bounded and which processes proceed inside and which outside that assumed community. We have, in

effect, created a little island; we study this island, and we usually conclude that the island is, in so many ways, an island. What
a bore. Let us think of some research projects that could provide
us with more interesting observations of multicultural realities
and that could also help bridge the gaping gulf between the two
heaps, the grand verbose theory and the detailed but unimagina-
tive empirical project. All the examples mentioned here are
currently in progress and have been awarded funding from various research councils or foundations. They are thus not pipe
dreams but feasible and fundable projects.

Unlike older streams of research, these new initiatives are not
coordinated from above but seek out their own directions of
flow. To bring some rough-and-ready order into their presenta-
tion, one may think of three general headings: the relationships
between nation-state cultures and "their" minorities, the relationships between and among minorities, and the processes that
reach across nation-state borders. I shall follow this order sys-
tematically to cut one possible path through the rich jungle of
up-to-date empirical research.

First, there are complex relationships between nation-state cultures and the so-called minorities that, note, they create for
themselves. Historians have shown time and again how Western
colonial powers imposed upon their subject peoples the very labels
of "majority" and "minority" and how they imposed, and sometimes invented, a whole range of boundaries: The creation of
majority and minority tribes, religions, castes, language communities, and even races was part and parcel of all colonial
administrations. In many of these cases, it was thus the Western
elites who created their own majority and minority problems
among the so-called tribes, races, and castes they had conquered
(Dirks 1989, 1996; Appadurai 1993; Fox 1995). Yet this process is
far from over: It continues apace every day, for cultural difference
is not given by nature, but created by social interaction. Student
researchers active in London's Southall have demonstrated this

clearly (McGarry 1990; Hawkes 1990; Yabsley 1990; see also Baumann 1996), and others are continuing this work. A new project in Southall aims precisely at "focusing research attention on those previously considered 'non-ethnic', and through this means understanding how and why ethnicity comes to be considered a determining characteristic of some groups and not others" (Robinson et al. 1997, 8; see also Turner 1998). This is not simply research on conceptualizations; it has an immediate social use— "to seek to understand how potential conflict is related to the ways that young (white) men define, understand themselves and behave as people with robust 'ethnic' or 'non-ethnic' identities" (Robinson et al. 1997, 8). This is important for two reasons. Practically, we need to understand those who hover at the cutting edge of racist violence, for racism is largely a problem created by so-called majorities, not so-called minorities. Intellectually, we need to understand how, why, and when conceptions of ethnicity, culture, and even race are reified or unreified. This is also the advice I have come to give most of my "ethnically Dutch" students in Amsterdam who want to do research on the multicultural future: Don't push your way into a suppressed minority whom you are not yet competent to understand. Study your own tribe, for it may be they who are "the multicultural problem."

This kind of research can also throw an entirely new and critical light on the social science literature itself. One Amsterdam student, Marisja de Best, has found out a crucial way of rereading the literature on Muslims in the Netherlands. Having done research among white Dutch emigrants in New Zealand, she found that the stereotypes that Dutch social researchers ascribed to the "backward Muslims" in the Netherlands apply, almost word for word, to the Dutch who sought a better future abroad. If such a study gets read by the Dutch who stayed at home, and be it in the form of a newspaper article, she will have opened up an important space for a more self-critical and self-reflexive discussion of "the multicultural problem" in the Netherlands.

The Multicultural Riddle

There are three other ways by which any serious student can advance our understanding of the links between a nation-state culture and "its" so-called minorities. They may be called the three Ms: the market, the media, and the *madrassa* (the Qur'anic word for "school"). Concerning the market, we have already touched upon the commercialization of ethnic and cultural difference in the shape of "red boots multiculturalism." The most original and also the most entertaining paper in this field was written by Ayse Caglar, then an M.A. student at Berlin (Caglar 1995). It deals with the *döner kebap,* that is, a portion of spit-roasted *halal* meat served in a pocket of Turkish flat bread (*pide*), garnished with salad and topped with garlic yogurt or hot dressings. In Germany, home to nearly two million Turks, the *döner kebap* figures as "*the* traditional ethnic food of Turks in the eyes of Germans" (p. 209), and it has become an enormously popular fast food in almost all German cities. Yet this "ethnic fast food" is anything but a traditional Turkish dish; rather, "*döner* (in the form offered in Germany) is itself a new and hybrid product" and "although produced and sold mostly by Turks and known as a Turkish food in Germany, *döner kebap* in the . . . [German] form is not available in Turkey" (pp. 209–10). Yet because of the strong, and exceptionally positive, associations that it has conferred on Turkishness, the *döner* has become a powerful symbol in the public debate about Germany as a cosmopolitan and multicultural country: It now "functions as an arena in which hostilities against and solidarity with Turks and foreigners are asserted" (p. 221). In this process, the hybrid little *döner* can even get transmogrified into an American-style "McKebap" or a higher-class "slim-line" or "health *döner*" (pp. 211, 226). A study such as Ayse Caglar's allows for a strategy that is as exciting to read as it is well grounded in empirical observation. It starts out with a material object which, on the face of it, looks perfectly matter of fact, and it spirals out from this item of "Turkish" fast food to encompass a vast transnational and pluricultural circle of

148

meaning-making, symbolic representations, and the renegotiation of so-called "cultural boundaries." This research strategy is as fresh as a kebap straight from the spitroast, more nourishing for theory than the usual junk-burgers of recycled abstractions, and can be used further by any imaginative student who has one semester's time to take a bite at the multicultural riddle.

From the first M, the market, to the second, the media, is but one step, sometimes less. Yet there are very few serious studies of media representations of the multicultural aspirations that the general public is presumed to share. The point was most forcefully driven home to me when, along with one thousand other people in a London cinema, I was waiting for *Sammy and Rosie Get Laid*, a film directed by Hanif Qureishi, the first Muslim director who gained access to mass audiences in Britain. While waiting, the audience was treated to a whole series of vaguely "multiculturalist advertisements," among them one that promised us sulky Mississippi riverside sex as the reward for buying a bottle of a vaguely Cajun liqueur. "Someone should study this," was my reaction then and has remained it since. Marie Gillespie's *Television, Ethnicity and Cultural Change* (1995) is the first good book that has empirically studied the workings of cinema and advertising, television and video as they work out among a so-called minority. This is an astonishing first, for there has been no shortage of theoretical stabs in the void of "ethnic perceptions" of popular and media culture. We need more social science students who tell us, in engaging detail and analytic precision, how the multicultural citizens of the future watch the commercial representations of perceived cultural difference. Why is Gillespie still the only one who compares observable people's reactions to an Indian-produced *Mahabharata*, as opposed to a self-consciously multicultural National Shakespeare Company production? Why has no one else compared observable Muslims' reaction to the CNN or BBC coverage of the Gulf War with the same people's reactions to Muslim satellite news programs?

Could it be that the social scientists paid for studying media representations find it easier to give us their own personal "readings" of "televisual texts," unspoiled by any interference from people without a degree? This would certainly save them the trouble of social research, for one can do that kind of thing in the comfort of one's favorite arm chair. The only trouble is that it steams itself up into a broiling haze of reboiled jargon, mixed with some meta-Nietzschean bits of para-Foucauldian agony on how complicated the world would be if everyone were as complex as me. One page is enough, and none might be better. TV research by narcissistic zapping and jotting may be great fun for some, but it is a waste unless it is based on interaction and in-depth interviews with the people we want to understand.

Strangely, things have not gotten better even after the media have meanwhile crossed all boundaries of national research traditions. When Oprah Winfrey gets people to discuss whether Tiger Woods is an African American, an American Thai, an African American Thai, or a multiethnic phenomenon, any media scientist should have something to document, no matter which country their informants watch Oprah from. A TV entertainer may well be content with asking the opinions of one or the other intellectual or community guru. Social researchers can do better than that: In taking up such false alternatives, they can seek the reactions of those who must build the multicultural future as they perceive it. We need to understand their reasonings, their motives, and the contexts within which they argue their points. Professors in TV armchair studies may, and hopefully will, drop dead with palsy from their own self-serving speculations. What we need are empirical experts on people's perceptions when they, that is, people, watch the box.

The third of the three Ms in this first stream of research was dubbed *madrassa*, the Arabic and generally Qur'anic word for "school." In researching the relationships between the nation-state culture and the so-called minority cultures that it produces, this sounds like an obvious linkage point. After all, it was the school as a state institution that laid the foundations of "national consciousness" in the nineteenth-century West. Without compulsory schooling for all, there would have been no Western nationalisms then, and without it, no nationalisms can be created now. This much Ernest Gellner (1983) has certainly got right. Yet obvious as the linkage point may be, it has only reached the multicultural research agenda very recently. One of the most interesting hypotheses about the relationship between the nation-state cultures and "their" minorities has come out of a research project that compares Turkish-born youths in four West European countries (Schiffauer et al. 1996).

At first sight, this kind of new project is outside the reach of a single student, or even a group of students looking for a project that is both new and feasible. Its hypothesis, however, that each nation-state is engaged, by means of its schools, in creating "its" minorities in its own image, can be researched even on the smallest scale. To put it simply, German schools create German-style Turks, French schools create French-style Turks, and the so-called problems that the German or French states see in the Turkish presence are in fact reflections of how these states run themselves, run their schools, and run the curricula. The steps that lead to this argument are familiar from chapters 3 and 4. Each Western nation-state has developed its own civil culture, that is, its own ways of *how* problems are discussed, *how* conflicts should be resolved, and *how* minority interests should be represented in accordance with *how* it defines the common good. It is through schools that the state imparts these styles of *how to* vis-à-vis nationals and foreigners alike, and it does so through both the explicit curricula and the implicit ones. Among the explicit curricula, one thinks of the teaching of history and the national language, of religious education and social studies. Among the implicit curricula, one thinks of the civic culture messages imparted through team sports or physical discipline or through the styles of discussion and self-representation that are favored or discouraged. The question to be answered now is this: How do the self-identifications of minority students respond to, and partly reflect, the styles of *how to* that are imparted at school?

At first sight, this is a complicated question, and the State, School and Ethnicity project is being pursued in four different countries to profile their different civic culture messages by mutual comparison. Yet when it comes to it, the empirical core of the project is nothing more complicated than fieldwork, participant observation, and interviews in and outside the classroom—a task that any degree student can take in hand for his or her social sciences project. What is new about such a project is that it no longer exoticizes the foreigner or the "second generation" of some "immigrant community." On the contrary, what it exoticizes, and what it aims to examine, is the Western nation-state and how it manages, through schools, to create and reshape "its" minorities in its very own image. I here conclude my discussion of the first major stream of new research, concerned with the relationships between nation-state cultures and "their" minorities.

A second stream of research concerns the relationships between and among different minorities. Two kinds of projects seem to me particularly suited to students with limited time and money. One of the most astonishing gaps in empirical multicultural research concerns the multitude of the "cultures of commitment" (Baumann 1996) that cut across national, religious, and ethnic identifications. By these cultures of commitment I mean networks and groups such as socialists, feminists, trade or labor unions, gays and lesbians, green or environmental activists—in short, all those groups and social networks that, consciously or inadvertantly, unite constituencies identified with different cultural roots. It is astonishing how little attention we pay to these groups, so I may be forgiven for quoting myself to press the point. It arose out of fieldwork in London's suburb Southall:

From Meaning to Practice: What Students Can Do

> The socialist and feminist networks ... are local minorities;
> yet there are several reasons why they deserve ethnographic
> attention. To start with, it is decidedly strange to read so many
> community studies in which no one local seems capable of fun-
> damental dissent and everyone seems engaged in reproducing
> the same, indiscriminately shared, ethnic culture.... Secondly,
> I take it as read that socialist or feminist convictions can estab-
> lish alternative cultures, that is, comprehensive systems of
> meaning-making with and about "others". Finally, even rela-
> tively small networks of dissenters can influence ideas of
> culture and community around them ... the counter-cultures
> of Southall socialists and feminists contribute to the agenda
> that Southallians at large have to face. (Baumann 1996, 158)

It is in these cultures of conviction that multicultural practices can be observed at their most creative, and here that they
achieve their greatest emancipation from the reifying discourses
of culture, community, and mutually exclusive identities. It
stands to reason that such groups will often include people of the
so-called majorities along with the so-called minorities and that
they will entail all kinds of innovative dialogue between and
among different minorities. These processes of exchange
between people of different diasporic constituencies can also be
observed on a far larger scale, and this lends itself well to two
students working together. The view that each national or religious or ethnic minority faces the so-called majority on its own
is surprisingly naive: It results from the researcher's choice of
boundaries and of what he or she is prepared to take notice of. It
is, once again, a case of cutting up the vast multicultural land-
scape into tiny islands of some supposedly bounded character.
That the opposite is the case can be seen from both theoretical
reflection and empirical observation, and these will round out
our review of the second stream of innovative research.

Theoretically, we know that the essence of pluralist societies
lies in their crosscutting cleavages: Remember our hypothetical

Mr. Essentialist. Empirically, we know from the many court cases and legal debates reported in the daily papers that any claim raised in the name of one minority affects the future of many other minorities. The Western nation-state, after all, seeks to formulate laws and procedures that apply to all citizens or even all residents alike. It does not always succeed in this, but this is certainly the preferred solution for its lawmakers and administrators.[1] This striving for a centralized uniformity of rights and procedures lies at the very root of translating citizens' or residents' demands into shared common rights, and it cannot fail to tie different minorities together. There is also, however, a converse process: a process of differentiation. Let us take an example from the Netherlands, where Muslim residents are divided into Moroccan and Turkish Muslims.

Various Moroccan Muslim organizations have demanded certain rights from the state, such as funding for Muslim schools and the training of Muslim clergy in state-funded universities. The Turkish Muslim organizations have chosen in the first case to back the demand, yet bitterly oppose the second, given their experience with the state-run training of Muslim clergy in Turkey. The net result will be selective alliances between constitutencies that, in the process of selecting the points of agreement, will push forward a process of mutual differentiation. These dynamics of exchange between different (sub)constituencies deserve far more research attention that they have had so far; at the same time, such studies demand time and partnerships for comparative research, and they will lend themselves better to collaborative projects than to individual ones. That said, a debate on a crosscutting alliance or a new differentiation can also be observed on the local level by a single student armed with no more than a notebook, a knowledge of the context, and the methodological and language competence.

The third stream of the new multicultural research is trying to push its flow across the nation-state boundaries. The code words for this are "transnationalism" and "globalization," which, like so many code words, mean just about nothing at first sight. By transnationalism we mean all the bonds that go across nation-state boundaries; by globalization we mean the world turning into what Marshall McLuhan (1962) first called "the global village"—or perhaps a global city with very different suburbs. Whatever the buzzwords, the transnationalism or globalization agenda show the same sad gap between jargonized general assertions and reliable empirical studies. In trying to close this gap, there is a vast range of studies that students or groups of students can engage in empirically. One can distinguish three planes of transnational or globalizing processes, and while it is certain that they all interact, each of them can be studied on such a small-scale basis as one or two extended families. The three planes can be called long-distance familism, political or religious transnationalism, and cross-diasporic exchange (van der Veer et al. 1997). Let us throw a glance at the empirical realities of each.

Long-distance familism stands for all the links that families of migrants maintain, or establish anew, with their folks "at home."[2] Initially, these tend to be economic bonds: Migrants send remittances, or they invest back home for their own benefit. This economy, however, is also a moral economy. It elevates or diminishes the moral status of everyone who takes part in it. It often enhances the status of precisely those people who have most to lose from the social upheavals of migration: the family fathers who insist on running their wives' and children's lives according to traditional and usually patriarchal rules (Pels 1994; de Swaan 1997). Often, women and the young are the first to get used to urban Western ideas and practices that stress gender equality and individual freedom, for these are the implicit curricula of most Western schools, state services, social work, youth work, and provisions for women (du Bois-Raymond et al. 1994). The moral economy of patriarchal relations gets upset, and long-distance familism is one way of counteracting these upsets. At the same time, the political and religious conflicts that migrants experience in the diaspora have grown more intense, and the same is true of many political and religious conflicts back home. This is where the processes of transnationalism reach a second, political and religious, plane.

The 1990s have faced Muslims with a dramatic polarization of political and religious tensions both *at* home in the West and *back* home in the Muslim world. Quite apart from supporting cousins back home or building a retirement bungalow to return to, Muslim migrants have entered manifold relationships with political and religious organizations that operate both back home and in the cities of the West. Moreover, the transnationalism of these relationships becomes much more involved: It is no longer restricted to old or new bonds with the country of origin. Rather, the activities or struggles of the same diaspora start crossing Western nation-state boundaries, too. A Turkish Muslim in the Netherlands will look to organizations in Germany to get his or her bearings on the current political or religious controversies; a Kurdish Turk in France will look to Kurdish Iraqis in London to find out at what juncture the national struggle stands. The organizations that embody these struggles compete for followings across Western state boundaries, and they often do their best to be as effective among young people and women as among the patriarchs.

The third plane of transnationalism and globalization crosses the most unexpected border of all: the boundary between one diaspora and another. What is involved in such cross-diasporic exchange is quite simple to start with. Different diasporas in the same Western nation-state discover that they face the same problems. In the Netherlands, to come back to our previous example, there is a Muslim diaspora of Moroccans and a Muslim diaspora of Turks. What the Dutch state gives to one of them it cannot withhold from the other, although they may not both desire the same thing. Recalling the earlier example, Turkish and Moroccan

From Meaning to Practice: What Students Can Do

Muslims agree on wanting state-financed Muslim schools, and they have got them, but they disagree on how far the Dutch state should control the training of Muslim clerics. The dialectics between cross-diasporic alliance and cross-diasporic differentiation can also be observed in the ethnic and national arenas of collective identities. What is good for the Kurdish Turks in Germany must also be good for the Kurdish Iraqis in the Netherlands. The cross-communication and cross-exchange among and across different diasporas is a truly globalizing process, and so far we have failed to study it empirically for the ten years past when it developed with an astonishing intensity and dynamism.

There is thus urgent and inspiring work to be done on all three planes of transnationalism or globalization: the transfamilial, the political or religious, and the cross-diasporic. The question is only who will do it. At first sight, this third stream of projects again looks forbidding to students. It all seems a little complex, even though it sounds perfectly real to anyone who reads a newspaper once a week. Yet the equation between complexity and scale is quite misleading. There is not a single study as yet of even one extended family's experiences of the three planes of transnationalism or globalization. A student who does this well—and it can be done within six months of research—would contribute enormously to a better understanding of how these buzzword processes actually work. The smaller the scale, the greater the precision; the less impressed by theoretical jargon, the more important the data.

If we want to take the step from "red boots" multiculturalism to a genuinely multicultural way of multirelational thinking and behaving, there are plenty of things we can do. No student of the social sciences who wants to contribute to these will be short of a project that is feasible, intellectually sound, and politically renewing. The first step, the one from dreaming to meaning, took three acts of rethinking the riddle of culture. The second step, from meaning to doing, is praxis—the finest challenge there is.

Notes

1. This nation-state striving for civil uniformity across reified cultural categories shows some astonishing exceptions, as I have tried to show in the case of Great Britain (Baumann 1995b). In Southall, the supposedly secular nation-state invited religious institutions to administer the most fundamental of its tasks: to turn residents into citizens. The strategy of devolving its secular powers to temples and mosques was effective and practical, yet it questions our commonsense faith in the nation-state as a neutral agency, far removed from approaching its citizens as religious believers.

2. I say "back home," rather than "at home" because migrants are, of course, at home where they live, that is, in the place to which they migrated. "Back home," too, may sound like a phrase that stresses the otherness of migrants, but the more polite or politically correct circumlocutions like "country of origin" are equally bad on that score. To my knowledge, there is, as yet, no social science term that avoids the othering implications of "back home." I therefore settle for the simplest phrase, one that is also used by many migrants themselves.

Further Reading

Caglar, Ayse. 1995. "*McDöner: Döner Kebap* and the Social Positioning Struggle of German Turks." Pp. 209–30 in *Marketing in a Multicultural World: Ethnicity, Nationalism, and Cultural Identity*, eds. J. A. Costa and G. J. Bamossy. London: Sage.

Gillespie, Marie. 1995. *Television, Ethnicity and Cultural Change.* New York: Routledge; esp. pp. 87–108, 109–41.

References

Surnames preceded by prepositions (e.g., de, du, van) are alphabetized by their first capital letter.

Al-Azmeh, Aziz. 1993. "Prologue: Muslim 'Culture' and the European Tribe." Pp. 1–17 in *Islams and Modernities*. London: Verso.

Alibhai, Yasmin. 1987. "A White Christmas." *New Society* 18 (December): 15–17.

Anderson, Benedict. 1983. *Imagined Communities: Reflections on the Origin and Spread of Nationalism*. London: Verso.

Appadurai, Arjun. 1993. "Number in the Colonial Imagination." Pp. 314–39 in *Orientalism and the Post-Colonial Predicament*, eds. C. Breckenridge and Peter van der Veer. Philadelphia: University of Pennsylvania Press.

Appiah, K. Anthony. 1994. "Identity, Authenticity, Survival: Multicultural Societies and Social Reproduction." Pp. 149–64 in *Multiculturalism: Examining the Politics of Recognition*, ed. A. Gutmann. Princeton, NJ: Princeton University Press.

Asad, Talal. 1993a. "Anthropological Conceptions of Religion: Reflections on Geertz." Pp. 27–54 in *Genealogies of Religion*, ed. T. Asad. Baltimore: Johns Hopkins University Press.

Asad, Talal. 1993b. "Multiculturalism and British Identity in the Wake of the Rushdie Affair." Pp. 239–268 in *Genealogies of Religion*, ed. T. Asad. Baltimore: Johns Hopkins University Press.

Bakhtin, M. M. 1984 [1929]. *Problems of Dostoyevsky's Poetics*, trans. Caryl Emerson. Minneapolis: University of Minnesota Press.

Banks, Marcus. 1996. *Ethnicity: Anthropological Constructions*. London: Routledge.

Banks, S. P. 1995. *Multicultural Public Relations*. London: Sage.

Barth, Fredrik (ed.). 1969. *Ethnic Groups and Boundaries: The Social Organization of Cultural Difference*. London: George Allen & Unwin.

Barth, Fredrik. 1994a. "Enduring and Emerging Issues in the Analysis of Ethnicity." Pp. 11–32 in *The Anthropology of Ethnicity: Beyond "Ethnic Groups and Boundaries,"* eds. H. Vermeulen and C. Govers. Amsterdam: Het Spinhuis.

Barth, Fredrik. 1994b. "A Personal View of Present Tasks and Priorities in Cultural and Social Anthropology." Pp. 349–61 in *Assessing Cultural Anthropology*, ed. R. Borofsky. New York: McGraw-Hill.

Bauböck, R. 1995. *Transnational Citizenship: Membership and Rights in International Migration*. Aldershot, England: Elgar.

Baumann, Gerd. 1990. "The Re-Invention of Bhangra: Social Change and Aesthetic Shifts among Punjabis in Britain." *The World of Music* 32 (2): 81–97.

Baumann, Gerd. 1992. "Ritual Implicates 'Others': Re-reading Durkheim in a Plural Society." Pp. 97–116 in *Understanding Rituals*, ed. D. de Coppet. London: Routledge.

Baumann, Gerd. 1995a. "Convergence and Encompassment: Two Dynamics of Syncretization in a Multi-Ethnic Part of London." Pp. 99–117 in *Post-Migration Ethnicity: De-essentializing Cohesion, Commitments, and Comparison*, eds. G. Baumann and T. Sunier. Amsterdam: Het Spinhuis.

Baumann, Gerd. 1995b. "Religious Migrants in Secular Britain? The State as an Agent of Religious Encorporation." *Etnofoor* 8 (2): 31–46.

Baumann, Gerd. 1995c. "Managing a Polyethnic Milieu: Kinship and Interaction in a London Suburb." *Journal of the Royal Anthropological Institute* (new series, incorporating *Man*) 1 (3): 1–17.

Baumann, Gerd. 1996. *Contesting Culture: Discourses of Identity in Multi-Ethnic London*. Cambridge: Cambridge University Press.

References

Baumann, Gerd. 1997. "Dominant and Demotic Discourses of Culture: Their Relevance to Multi-Ethnic Alliances." Pp. 209–25 in *Debating Cultural Hybridity: Multi-Cultural Identities and the Politics of Racism*, eds. P. Werbner and T. Modood. London: Zed Books.

Bayrou, Francois. 1994. "Directive aux Chefs d'Etablissement." *Le Figaro* (September 21): 3.

Bellah, Robert. 1966. "Civil Religion in America." *Daedalus: Journal of the American Academy of Arts and Sciences* 95: 1–21.

Benson, Susan. 1981. *Ambiguous Ethnicity: Interracial Families in London.* Cambridge: Cambridge University Press.

Berger, Peter, and Thomas Luckmann. 1967. *The Social Construction of Reality: A Treatise in the Sociology of Knowledge.* Harmondsworth, England: Penguin Books.

Bernal, Martin. 1987. *Black Athena: The Afroasiatic Roots of Classical Civilization, I: The Fabrication of Ancient Greece, 1785–1895.* London: Free Association Books.

Bernal, Martin. 1991. *Black Athena: The Afroasiatic Roots of Classical Civilization, II: The Archaeological and Documentary Evidence.* London: Free Association Books.

Bhabha, H. K. 1994. *The Location of Culture.* London: Routledge.

Bhachu, Parminder. 1985. *Twice Migrants. East African Sikh Settlers in Britain.* London: Tavistock.

Black, Les. 1996. *New Ethnicities and Urban Culture: Racisms and Multiculture in Young Lives.* London: University College London Press.

Blacking, John. 1972. *Man and Fellowman* (Inaugural Lecture, The Queen's University of Belfast New Lecture Series 71). Belfast: The Queen's University.

du Bois-Raymond, Manuela, et al. 1994. *Kinderleben. Modernisierung von Kindheit im interkulturellen Vergleich.* Opladen, Germany: Leske & Budrich.

Borofsky, Robert (ed.). 1994. *Assessing Cultural Anthropology.* New York: McGraw-Hill.

Brah, Avtar. 1987. "Women of South Asian Origin in Britain: Issue and Concerns." *South Asia Research* 1 (1): 39–54.

Caglar, Ayse. 1995. *"McDöner: Döner Kebap* and the Social Positioning Struggle of German Turks." Pp. 209–30 in *Marketing in a Multicultural World: Ethnicity, Nationalism, and Cultural Identity*, eds. J. A. Costa and G. J. Bamossy. London: Sage.

Clifford, James. 1988. *The Predicament of Culture: Twentieth-Century Ethnography, Literature, and Art*. Cambridge: Harvard University Press.

Comaroff, John, and Jean Comaroff. 1992. *Ethnography and the Historical Imagination*. Boulder, Col.: Westview Press.

Connor, Walker. 1993. "Beyond Reason: The Nature of the Ethnonational Bond." *Ethnic and Racial Studies* 16 (3): 373–89.

Conway, Moncure Daniel (ed.). 1967. *The Writings of Thomas Paine, Volume II*. New York: AMS Press.

Costa, Janeen Arnold, and Gary J. Bamossy (eds.). 1995. *Marketing in a Multicultural World: Ethnicity, Nationalism, and Cultural Identity*. London: Sage.

Dembour, Marie-Benedicte. 1996. "Human Rights Talk and Anthropological Ambivalence: The Particular Contexts of Universal Claims." Pp. 18–39 in *Inside and Outside the Law*, ed. O. Harris. London: Routledge.

Dirks, Nicholas. 1989. "The Invention of Caste: Civil Society in Colonial India." *Social Analysis* 25: 42–51.

Dirks, Nicholas. 1996. "The Conversion of Caste: Location, Translation, and Appropriation." Pp. 115–36 in *Conversion to Modernities: The Globalization of Christianities*, ed. P. van der Veer. New York: Routledge.

Donald, J., and A. Rattansi (eds.). 1992. *"Race", Culture and Difference*. London: Sage Publications in association with The Open University.

Donnelly, Jack. 1982. "Human Rights and Human Dignity: An Analytic Critique of Non-Western Conceptions of Human Rights." *American Political Science Review* 76 (2): 303–16.

Donnelly, Jack. 1985. *The Concept of Human Rights*. New York: St. Martin's Press.

Donnelly, Jack. 1989. *Universal Human Rights in Theory and Practice*. Ithaca, NY: Cornell University Press.

Durkheim, Emile. [1893] 1947. *Suicide*. New York: Glencoe.

References

Durkheim, Emile. [1915] 1971. *The Elementary Forms of the Religious Life*, trans. J. W. Swain. London: George Allen & Unwin.

Eriksen, Thomas Hylland. 1992. *Us and Them in Modern Societies: Ethnicity and Nationalism in Trinidad, Mauritius and Beyond*. Oslo: Scandinavian University Press.

Eriksen, Thomas Hylland. 1993. *Ethnicity and Nationalism. Anthropological Perspectives*. London and Boulder, Col.: Pluto Press.

Eriksen, Thomas Hylland. 1998. *Communicating Cultural Difference and Identity: Ethnicity and Nationalism in Mauritius*. Oslo: Oslo University Occasional Papers in Social Anthropology. (For a more easily accessible update, see Eriksen 1992.)

Evans-Pritchard, E. E. 1940. *The Nuer*. Oxford: Clarendon Press.

Evans-Pritchard, E. E. 1951. *Nuer Kinship*. Oxford: Clarendon Press.

Fox, Richard. 1985. *Lions of the Punjab: Culture in the Making*. Berkeley and Los Angeles: University of California Press.

Furnivall, J. S. 1939. *Netherlands India: A Study of Plural Economy*. Cambridge, England: The University Press.

Furnivall, J. S. 1948. *Colonial Policy and Practice*. London: Cambridge University Press.

Gardell, Mattias. 1996. *Countdown to Armageddon: Louis Farrakhan and the Nation of Islam*. London: Hurst.

Geertz, Clifford. 1986. "The Uses of Diversity." *Michigan Quarterly Review* 25 (1): 105–23.

Gehrig, Gail. 1981. *American Civil Religion: An Assessment*. Storrs, Conn.: Society for the Scientific Study of Religion.

Gellner, Ernest. 1983. *Nations and Nationalism*. Oxford: Basil Blackwell.

Gillespie, Marie. 1989. "Technology and Tradition: Audio-Visual Culture among South Asian Families in West London." *Cultural Studies* III (2): 226–40.

Gillespie, Marie. 1995. *Television, Ethnicity and Cultural Change: An Ethnographic Study of Punjabi Londoners*. London: Routledge.

Gilroy, Paul. 1987. *There Ain't No Black in the Union Jack: The Cultural Politics of Race and Nation*. London: Routledge.

Gilroy, Paul. 1992. "The End of Antiracism." Pp. 49–61 in *"Race", Culture and Difference*, eds. J. Donald and A. Rattansi. London: Sage.

Glazer, Nathan, and Daniel P. Moynihan. 1963. *Beyond the Melting Pot.* Cambridge, Mass.: MIT Press.

Glick Schiller, N., L. Basch, and C. Blanc-Szanton (eds.). 1992. *Towards a Transnational Perspective on Migration: Race, Class, Ethnicity, and Nationalism Reconsidered.* New York: New York Academy of Sciences.

Goldberg, D. T. (ed.). 1994. *Multiculturalism: A Critical Reader.* Oxford: Blackwell.

van Gunsteren, H. 1994. "Four Conceptions of Citizenship." Pp. 36–48 in *The Condition of Citizenship*, ed. B. van Steenbergen. London: Sage.

Haaland, Gunnar. 1969. "Economic Determinants in Ethnic Processes." Pp. 58–73 in *Ethnic Groups and Boundaries: The Social Organization of Culture Difference*, ed. Fredrik Barth. London: George Allen & Unwin.

Habermas, Jurgen. 1994. "Citizenship and National Identity." Pp. 20–35 in *The Condition of Citizenship*, ed. B. van Steenbergen. London: Sage.

Hall, Stuart. 1991. "Old and New Identities, Old and New Ethnicities." Pp. 41–68 in *Culture, Globalization and the World-System*, ed. A. D. King. Basingstoke, England: Macmillan.

Hall, Stuart. 1992. "New Ethnicities." In *"Race", Culture and Difference*, eds. J. Donald and A. Rattansi. London: Sage.

Hamilton, Alexander, John Jay, and James Madison. 1937. *The Federalist: A Commentary on the Constitution of the United States.* New York: The Modern Library.

Handler, Richard. 1984. "On Sociocultural Discontinuity: Nationalism and Cultural Objectification in Quebec." *Current Anthropology* 25 (1): 55–71.

Handler, Richard. 1988. *Nationalism and the Politics of Culture in Quebec.* Madison: University of Wisconsin Press.

Harrison, P. 1990. *"Religion" and the Religions in the English Enlightenment.* Cambridge: Cambridge University Press.

Hawkes, Barbara. 1990. *Southall: An Ethnography of Change.* B.Sc. dissertation in Sociology, Uxbridge, England, Brunel University.

References

Heiberg, Marianne. 1989. *The Making of the Basque Nation*. Cambridge: Cambridge University Press.

Henkin, Louis. 1990. *The Age of Rights*. New York: Columbia University Press.

Hewitt, Roger. 1986. *White Talk Black Talk: Inter-Racial Friendship and Communication Amongst Adolescents*. Cambridge: Cambridge University Press.

Ho Chi Minh. 1967. *On Revolution: Selected Writings 1920–1966*, ed. Bernard Fall. New York: New American Library.

Hoffman, Stanley. 1993. "Thoughts on the French Nation Today." *Daedalus: Journal of the American Academy of Arts and Sciences* 122 (3): 63–80.

Hundleby, Richard. 1987. "A Place for Everyone? A Report on Afro-Caribbean Cultural Provisions in Southall." Research report, Department of Human Sciences, Brunel, The University of West London.

Hutchinson, John, and Anthony Smith (eds.). 1996. *Ethnicity*. Oxford: Clarendon Press.

Ignatieff, Michael. 1992. "Why 'Community' Is a Dishonest Word." *The Observer*, 3 May 1992, 7.

Jenkins, Richard. 1994. "Rethinking Ethnicity: Identity, Categorization, and Power." *Ethnic and Racial Studies* 17: 197–223.

Jenkins, Richard. 1997. *Rethinking Ethnicity: Arguments and Explorations*. London: Sage.

Johansson, E. 1981. "The History of Literacy in Sweden, in Comparison with Some Other Countries." Pp. 151–82 in *Literacy and Social Development in the West: A Reader*, ed. H. J. Graff. Cambridge: Cambridge University Press.

Kalka, Iris. 1991. "Striking a Bargain. Political Radicalism in a Middle-class London Borough." Pp. 203–25 in *Black and Ethnic Leaderships in Britain: The Cultural Dimensions of Political Action*, eds. P. Werbner and M. Anwar. London: Routledge.

Kandre, P. 1967. "Autonomy and Integration of Social Systems: The Iu Mien (Yao) Mountain Population and Their Neighbours." In *Southeast Asian Tribes, Minorities, and Nations*, ed. P. Kunstadter. Princeton, NJ: Princeton University Press.

Kapferer, Bruce. 1988. *Legends of People, Myths of State: Violence, Intolerance and Political Culture in Sri Lanka and Australia.* Washington, D.C.: Smithsonian Institution Press.

Kasinitz, Philip (ed.). 1996. *Metropolis: Centre and Symbol of Our Times.* London: Macmillan.

Keesing, Roger. 1994. "Theories of Culture Revisited." Pp. 301–10 in *Assessing Cultural Anthropology*, ed. R. Borofsky. New York: McGraw-Hill.

Kepel, Gilles. 1996. *Allah in the West: Islamic Movements in America and Europe.* Cambridge: Polity.

King, Martin Luther. [1963] 1968. "I Have a Dream." *The Negro History Bulletin* 31 (May 1968): 16–17.

Kitto, H. D. F. 1951. *The Greeks: A Study of the Character and History of an Ancient Civilization, and of the People Who Created It.* Harmondsworth, England: Pelican.

Kobayashi, Audrey. 1993. "Multiculturalism: Representing a Canadian Institution." Pp. 205–31 in *Place/Culture/Representation*, eds. J. Duncan and D. Ley. London: Routledge.

Kuper, Adam. 1977. *The Social Anthropology of Radcliffe-Brown.* London: Routledge.

Kymlicka, W. 1995a. *Multicultural Citizenship.* Oxford: Clarendon Press.

Kymlicka, W. (ed.). 1995b. *The Rights of Minority Cultures.* London: Oxford University Press.

Larson, Heidi. 1989. "Asian Children—British Childhood." Ph.D. thesis, Department of Anthropology, The University of California, Berkeley.

Leach, Edmund. 1976. *Culture and Communication: The Logic by which Symbols are Connected.* Cambridge: Cambridge University Press.

Lefkowitz, Mary R. 1996. *Not Out of Africa: How Afrocentrism Became an Excuse to Teach Myth as History.* New York: Basic Books.

Lefkowitz, Mary R., and Guy MacLean Rogers (eds.). 1996. *Black Athena Revisited.* Chapel Hill: University of North Carolina Press.

Leveau, Remy. 1988. "The Islamic Presence in France." Pp. 107–22 in *The New Islamic Presence in Western Europe*, eds. T. Gerholm and Y. Lithman. London: Mansell.

References

Levi-Strauss, Claude. 1964. *Totemism*. London: Merlin Press.

Livingstone, F. B., and T. Dobzhansky. 1962. "On the Non-Existence of Human Races." *Current Anthropology* 3: 279–81.

Lutz, Catherine, and Lila Abu-Lughod (eds.). 1990. *Language and the Politics of Emotion*. Cambridge: Cambridge University Press.

Magida, Arthur. 1996. *Prophet of Rage: A Life of Louis Farrakhan and His Nation*. New York: Basic Books.

Mann, Michael. 1986. *The Sources of Social Power, Vol. I: A History of Power from the Beginning to A.D. 1760*. Cambridge: Cambridge University Press.

Marshall, Thomas Humphrey. 1965. *Class, Citizenship, and Social Development: Essays*. Garden City, NY: Doubleday.

McCloud, Aminah Beverly. 1995. *African American Islam*. New York: Routledge.

McDermott, Mustafa Yusuf, and Muhammad Manazir Ahsan. 1979. *The Muslim Guide for Teachers, Employers, Community Workers and Social Administrators in Britain*. London: The Islamic Foundation.

McDonald, Maryon. 1986. "Celtic Ethnic Kinship and the Problem of Being English." *Current Anthropology* 27 (4): 333–47.

McDonald, Maryon. 1989. *"We Are Not French!" Language, Culture and Identity in Brittany*. London: Routledge.

McGarry, Teresa. 1990. "A Study of 'The Irish' in Southall." B.Sc. dissertation in Sociology, 2 vols. Uxbridge, England: Brunel University.

McLuhan, Marshall. 1962. *The Gutenberg Galaxy*. Toronto: Toronto University Press.

Mead, George Herbert. 1934. *Mind, Self, and Society*. Chicago: University of Chicago Press.

Mitchell, J. Clyde. 1956. *The Kalela Dance: Aspects of Social Relationships among Urban Africans in Northern Rhodesia*. Rhodes-Livingstone Papers, no. 27. Manchester: Manchester University Press.

Morris, H. S. 1968. *The Indians in Uganda*. London: Weidenfeld & Nicolson.

Nietzsche, Friedrich. [1878] 1968. *Menschliches, Allzumenschliches. Ein Buch fur freie Geister*. ed. Hans Heinz Holz. Frankfurt: Fischer.

Patten, John. 1989a. "The Muslim Community in Britain." *The Times* (July 7): 3.

Patten, John. 1989b. "On Being British." Mimeograph, London, H. M. Home Office (July 18).

Pels, Trees (ed.). 1994. *Opvoeding in Chinese, Marokkaanse en Surinaam-Creoolse Gezinnen.* Rotterdam: ISEO.

Phoenix, Ann. 1988. "Narrow Definitions of Culture: The Case of Early Motherhood." In *Enterprising Women: Ethnicity, Economy, and Gender Relations,* eds. S. Westwood and P. Bhachu. London: Routledge.

Pryce, Ken. 1979. *Endless Pressure: A Study of West Indian Life-Styles in Bristol.* Bristol: Bristol Classical Press.

Radcliffe-Brown, R. R. 1924. *Structure and Function in Primitive Society.* London: Cohen & West.

Rampton, B. 1995. *Crossing: Language and Ethnicity among Adolescents.* London: Longman.

Rath, Jan, Kees Groenendijk, and Rinus Penninx. 1991. "The Recognition of Islam in Belgium, Great Britain and the Netherlands." *New Community* 1: 101–14.

Rex, John, and B. Drury (eds.). 1994. *Ethnic Mobilisation in a Multi-Cultural Europe.* Aldershot: Avebury.

Robinson, Ian, Ronald Frankenberg, and Aaron Turner. 1997. *Reconsidering Ethnicity: A Study of "Non-Ethnic" People in the Midst of Ethnicity.* Research proposal submitted to the Economic and Social Research Council. Uxbridge, England: Brunel University.

van Rooden, Peter. 1996. "Secularization and De-Christianization in the Netherlands." Pp. 131–153 in *Säkulariserung, Dechristianisierung und Rechristianisierung im neuzeitlichen Europa: Bilanz und Perspektiven der Forschung,* ed. H. Lehmann. Göttingen, Germany: Vandenhoeck & Ruprecht.

Rosaldo, Renato. 1989. *Culture and Truth: The Remaking of Social Analysis.* Boston: Beacon Press.

Rothschild, Joseph. 1981. *Ethnopolitics: A Conceptual Framework.* New York: Columbia University Press.

References

Sahlins, Marshall. 1994. "Goodbye to Tristes Tropes: Ethnography in the Context of Modern World History." Pp. 377–94 in *Assessing Cultural Anthropology*, ed. R. Borofsky. New York: McGraw-Hill.

Said, Edward. 1978. *Orientalism*. London: Routledge & Kegan Paul.

Said, Edward. 1989. "Representing the Colonized: Anthropology and Its Interlocutors." *Critical Inquiry* 15: 205–25.

Samad, Yunas. 1992. "Book Burning and Race Relations: Political Mobilisation of Bradford Muslims." *New Community* 18 (4): 507–19.

Schiffauer, Werner. 1988. "Migration and Religiousness." Pp. 146–58 in *The New Islamic Presence in Western Europe*, eds. T. Gerholm and Y. Lithman. London: Mansell.

Schiffauer, Werner. 1993. "Die *civil society* und der Fremde— Grenzmarkierungen in Vier Politischen Kulturen." Pp. 185–99 in *Schwierige Fremdheit. Ueber Untegration und Ausgrenzung in Einwanderungslandern*, eds. F. Balke et al. Frankfurt/Main: Fischer.

Schiffauer, Werner. 1995. "Islamischer Fundamentalismus—Zur Konstruktion des Radikal Anderen." *Neue Politische Literatur* 40 (1): 95–105.

Schiffauer, Werner, et al. 1996. "State, School and Ethnicity: The Relationship between National Civic Culture and Minority Identifications, Compared among Turkish Youth in France, Britain, the Netherlands and Germany." Research proposal submitted to the Volkswagen Stiftung. Frankfurt (Oder), Germany: European University Viadrina, mimeograph.

Schlesinger, Arthur. 1991. *The Disuniting of America: Reflections on a Multicultural Society*. New York: W. W. Norton.

Shadid, W. A. R., and P. S. Koningsveld. 1991. *The Integration of Islam and Hinduism in Europe*. Kampen, The Netherlands: Pharos.

Soysal, Y. N. 1994. *Limits of Citizenship: Migrants and Postnational Membership in Europe*. Chicago: University of Chicago Press.

van Steenbergen, B. (ed.). 1994. *The Condition of Citizenship*. London: Sage.

Sunier, Thijl. 1995. "Moslims in Nederland, Nederlandse Moslims: Sociale Integratie in de sfeer van de Islam." Pp. 180–204 in *Sferen van Integratie. Naar een Gedifferencieerd Allochtonenbeleid*, eds. G. Engbersen and R. Gabriels. Amsterdam, The Netherlands: Boom.

Sunier, Thijl. 1996. *Islam in Beweging. Turkse Jongeren en Islamitische Organisaties.* Amsterdam, The Netherlands: Het Spinhuis.

de Swaan, Abram. 1981. "The Politics of Agoraphobia." *Theory and Society* (May): 359–86.

de Swaan, Abram. 1988. *In Care of the State: Healthcare, Education and Welfare in Europe and the USA in the Modern Era.* Cambridge: Polity.

de Swaan, Abram. 1997. "Over Onzekerheden in de Verschuiving van Bevels—Naar Onderhandelinshuishouding." Pp. 5–9 in *Gezin en Beleid. Jaarboek Nederlandse Gezinsraad.* Utrecht, The Netherlands: De Tijdstroom.

Taylor, Charles. 1994. "The Politics of Recognition." Pp. 25–74 in *Multiculturalism: Examining the Politics of Recognition,* ed. A. Gutmann. Princeton, NJ: Princeton University Press.

Turner, Aaron. 1998. "Taking Issue with the Irrelevant: Multi-Situated Fieldwork re: Young White Males." Paper delivered at the Sixth Biannual Conference of the European Association of Social Anthropologists, Frankfurt/Main, Germany.

Turner, Bryan. 1994. "Postmodern Culture/Modern Citizens." Pp. 153–68 in *The Condition of Citizenship,* ed. B. van Steenbergen. London: Sage.

Turner, Terence. 1993. "Anthropology and Multiculturalism: What Is Anthropology That Multiculturalists Should Be Mindful of It?" *Cultural Anthropology* 8 (4): 411–29.

Vayda, Andrew. 1994. "Actions, Variations and Change: The Emerging Anti-Essentialist View in Anthropology." Pp. 320–29 in *Assessing Cultural Anthropology,* ed. R. Borofsky. New York: McGraw-Hill.

van der Veer, Peter. 1994. "The Novel and Rushdie's Novel." Pp. 179–91 in *Religious Nationalism: Hindus and Muslims in India.* Berkeley and Los Angeles: University of California Press.

van der Veer, Peter (ed.). 1995. *Nation and Migration: The Politics of Space in the South Asian Diaspora.* Philadelphia: University of Pennsylvania Press.

van der Veer, Peter, et al. 1997. "Transnationalism: A Three-Level Comparative Approach. Transfamilism, Politico-Religious Transnation-

References

alism, and Cross-Diasporic Dynamics among Turks and Moroccans in the Netherlands." Project application submitted to NWO, The Hague. Amsterdam, The Netherlands: Research Centre Religion and Society.

Verma, Gajendra. 1990. "Pluralism: Some Theoretical and Practical Considerations." Pp. 44–57 in *Britain: A Plural Society. Report of a Seminar*. London: Commission for Racial Equality, Discussion Papers 3.

Vertovec, Stephen. 1992. "Community and Congregation in London Hindu Temples: Divergent Trends." *New Community* 18 (2): 251–64.

Vertovec, Stephen. 1994. "Multicultural, Multi-Asian, Multi-Muslim Leicester: Dimensions of Social Complexity, Ethnic Organization, and Local Government Interface." *Innovation* 7 (3): 259–76.

Vertovec, Stephen. 1995. "Hindus in Trinidad and Britain: Ethnic Religion, Reification, and the Politics of Public Space." Pp. 132–156 in *Nation and Migration: The Politics of Space in the South Asian Diaspora*, ed. P. van der Veer. Philadelphia: University of Pennsylvania Press.

Vertovec, Stephen (ed.). 1997. *Muslim European Youth: Re-producing Religion, Ethnicity and Culture*. Aldershot, England: Avebury.

Vertovec, Stephen, and Ceri Peach (eds.). 1997. *Islam in Europe and the Politics of Religion and Community*. Basingstoke, England: Macmillan.

Waardenburg, Jacques. 1988. "The Institutionalization of Islam in the Netherlands, 1961–86." Pp. 8–31 in *The New Islamic Presence in Western Europe*, eds. T. Gerhold and Y. Lithman. London: Mansell.

Wallman, Sandra (ed.). 1979. *Ethnicity at Work*. London: Macmillan.

Weber, Max. 1930. *The Protestant Ethic and the Spirit of Capitalism*. London: Routledge & Kegan Paul.

Weber, Max. 1978. *Economy and Society: An Outline of Interpretive Sociology*, ed. G. Roth and C. Wittich. Berkeley and Los Angeles: University of California Press.

Werbner, Pnina. 1990. *The Migration Process: Capital, Gifts and Offerings among British Pakistanis*. Oxford: Berg.

Werbner, Pnina, and Tariq Modood (eds.). 1997. *Debating Cultural Hybridity*. London: Sage.

Williams, Raymond. 1976. *Keywords: A Vocabulary of Culture and Society*. London: Fontana.

Wilson, William J. 1987. *The Truly Disadvantaged: The Inner City, the Underclass, and Public Policy.* Chicago: The University of Chicago Press.

Worsley, Peter. 1984. *The Three Worlds: Culture and World Development.* London: Weidenfeld and Nicholson.

Yabsley, Hazel. 1990. "Proximity: Processes of Ethnicity and Community Explored in Southall." B.Sc. dissertation in Sociology and Social Anthropology, 4 vols. Uxbridge, England: Brunel University.

Young, Iris Marion. 1989. "Polity and Group Difference: A Critique of the Ideal of Universal Citizenship." *Ethics* 99: 250–74.

Young, Iris Marion. 1990. *Justice and the Politics of Difference.* Princeton, NJ: Princeton University Press.

Yuval-Davis, N. 1992. "Fundamentalism, Multiculturalism and Women in Britain." Pp. 278–91 in *"Race", Culture and Difference,* eds. J. Donald and A. Rattansi. London: Sage.

Index

Compound terms are alphabetized by their first word, thus: civil religion, Nation of Islam, methodological individualism.

Index

Index

Sahlins, M. 96
Samad, Y. 73
Schiffauer, W. 45–7, 73–4, 80, 130, 151–2
school 37–8, 49–51, 150–1, 157
secularism 13, 22, 41–55, 76–8, 158
sexuality 5, 7–8, 15, 118, 120, 127, 141, 144
Sikh 47, 121–34
Smith, A. 27
socialism 35, 46, 152–3
social services 32–3, 46, 77, 155
soldiers 19, 35, 44, 113
South Africa 60–2, 104, 120
Southall 57–8, 121–34, 158
sovereignty 19, 30, 35, 113
Soysal, Y.N. 144
Steenbergen, B. van 106
Sunier, T. 103
Swaan, A. de 19, 35, 155
Sweden 37

Taylor, C. 80, 106–20
television 38–9, 45, 95, 128, 149–50
Tito, B. 54
tourism 82–3
transnationalism 155–8
Turkish 12, 47, 52, 65, 73–4, 148–9, 154
Turner, A. 147
Turner, B. 144
Turner, T. 88–9, 96, 105–6, 123

United Nations 4, 6, 19, 35, 44, 113
United States 1–3, 8–10, 18, 34, 38, 42–6, 51–4, 74–6, 127
urbanization 10, 35, 37, 73–4, 81–2

Vayda, A. 96
Veer, P. van der 69, 71–2, 79, 96, 155
Verma, G. 97, 99–100
Vertovec, S. 96, 131
Vietnam 29, 42, 44

Wallman, S. 80
Washington, G. 43
Weber, M. 25, 61, 68
welfare 5, 32–3, 36, 46–8, 77, 85, 155
Werbner, P. 80, 96
whites 57–8, 79, 81–3, 147; *see also* ethnicity
Wilson, W. J. 9
Winfrey, O. 150
women 15, 39, 66–8, 75, 80, 144, 152–3
Woods, T. 150

Yabsley, H. 133, 147
Young, I.M. 144–5
Yugoslavia 14, 52, 54, 79

Zambia 58